A Fool's Guide to Clowning

Leslie Ann Akin

Global Touch Press
Lake Oswego, Oregon

Global Touch Press
Lake Oswego, Oregon

ISBN: 978-1-7327776-0-6
Printed in the United States of America
Second edition
Editing by Dena Piraino

Dedicated to my loving husband Ron Akin

In memory of Steve Rancatore

Thank You

To my mother Suzanne Corley, my biggest encourager and cheerleader.

My awesome daughter Lisa Homann, for assisting with props and the live bunny.

Cathy Gibbons, editor of *Laugh-Makers Magazine* who asked me to write a column in its second year of publication. She recognized something in me I did not see in myself. I am forever grateful.

John Kennedy for mentoring with close-up magic lessons and performance advice.

Thank you for your friendships and inspiration over the years: Cathy and Bob Gibbons, Dena Piraino, Barry "Bonzo" DeChant, Danson Hanson, Daren Dundee, and Bruce "Charlie" Johnson.

Foreword

Cathy Gibbons

As editor of *Laugh-Makers Variety Arts Magazine* I was always on the lookout for talented performers. When I first saw Leslie Akin perform as Flower T. Clown, I knew she had "it"—that elusive combination of charisma, enthusiasm, confidence and professionalism. Most of all, she made me laugh. I was glad she agreed to share her good ideas in a column for Laugh-Makers, and am glad now that she has gathered, expanded and added new material in this book for a new generation of readers. You are sure to find many gems in this special book.

Bruce 'Charlie' Johnson

The best clowns learn from each other. It has been said that a smart person learns from their mistakes and a wise person learns from the mistakes of others. By listening to others, you can learn what they discovered through trial and error without having to make the same mistakes yourself. That gives you an advantage. You start by building upon the foundation they have laid so you start further ahead of where they began. Then you can discover more wisdom by making your own unique mistakes.

Not only do the best clowns exchange wisdom, they exchange ideas which leads to more ideas. Frequently when I share an idea with somebody else, they see something about the idea that I had overlooked. It inspires them to create a new idea. When they share their new idea with me, I see something that they had not realized was there. That inspires a third idea that neither of us would have thought of on our own.

Modern technology has made instructional videos easy to obtain, but reading remains my favorite method of learning. Reading triggers your brain to create images. This exercises your ability to visualize.

Visualization is an important part of creativity. Watching a video does not trigger the same response because the image is already created for you. It prevents you from exercising your own visualization. In addition, it locks you into the originator's vision because it can be hard to break such a clear visual memory. If you visualize something on your own, it is formed in a way that best suits your personality and style. Your own images are often superior to those provided by others. So, I applaud your decision to learn by reading this book.

I first got to know Leslie through her writing. In February 1982, the *Laugh-Makers Variety Arts Magazine,* published by

Bob Gibbons and edited by Cathy Gibbons, was introduced. It was a magazine devoted to family entertainment and eclectic performance styles. Nothing like it had appeared in print before. It was fresh and exciting.

A year later, Leslie became one of the Laugh-Makers magazine columnists. My Laugh-Makers column debuted a few months later. When I received each new issue, the first thing I did was turn to my article. I was still a new enough author that it was a thrill to see my words in print. Usually the second thing I did was turn to Leslie's article. I always found it thought provoking.

Soon, Leslie and I became pen pals. We started by writing to each other commenting on the articles that had appeared in the latest issue. Then our letters began to include a discussion of the writing process. Bouncing ideas off each other improved our articles.

I met Leslie in person when she was touring with the All-American Circus. I visited the show when they performed in Southern California, and saw one of her first circus performances.

Being columnists for *Laugh-Makers Variety Arts Magazine* opened many doors to us. One of the most important was being on staff for Clown Camp and the Laugh-Makers Variety Arts Conferences.

The first Laugh-Makers Conference was held in 1986. It was a thrilling experience. Most of the Laugh-Makers columnists were meeting in person for the first time. Reading everyone's articles had led to a great deal of mutual respect between staff members. Many of us were the most experienced entertainers in our home town, and were usually called upon to teach the local classes. While an instructor can, and should, learn from their students, this was the first time we had the opportunity to attend a class and simply be a student. We eagerly sat in on each other's classes. I took every class taught by Leslie that I could fit into my schedule. Not only did I learn more about clowning, but I studied what she did as an instructor. Now our letters began to include thoughts about teaching variety arts. That exchange helped me become a better instructor.

In recognition of her contributions to the magazine and conferences, Bob and Cathy named Leslie their first Laugh-Makers Contributor of the Year. It was a richly deserved honor. When it was announced at the first Laugh-Makers Conference, Leslie was given a standing ovation.

At the Laugh-Makers Variety Arts Conferences, I got to see Leslie performing as Flower T. Clown. I was charmed by her character and entertained by her routines.

Leslie's routines have been performed by many other entertainers. Although our performance styles are very different, I have been able to include material in my repertoire that was inspired by her routines. While you can create your own variation of a routine so that it fits your style, many clowns just copy what they have seen. The problem is that a copy is always inferior to the original, especially when it is a copy of a copy. I compare it to photocopying. With each generation of photo copies, the fine details become blurred and little flaws become enlarged. When each generation of a copied routine, the details that originally made it entertaining are forgotten and changes are perpetuated that make the routine less successful.

In this book, you get to return to the original routines that Leslie created and use that as the basis for your own performances.

I am honored to once again have something that I have written appear in the same publication as Leslie's writing. I hope that you benefit as much from her writing as I have. I hope someday to see you perform something inspired by what you read here.

Barry 'Bonzo' DeChant

Clowning is a very specific art form, which requires many hours, days, months, even years of training. Clowns are very possessive of their art. They look despairingly at those we call home town clowns, who sometimes scare little ones (and big ones). True clowns are professionals in their work. They study with professionals.

They purchase books like this one, written by a very professional clown, Leslie Ann Akin, Flower T. Clown. I've known Leslie Ann for many years and have a great deal of respect for her and her clown persona. We clowned together many times at many places. Perhaps the most notable was The White House Easter Egg Roll in 1986 when our President was Ronald Reagan.

We entertained hundreds of children as they played on the White House lawn. Those were the days. But Wait. That's not all a clown does. Flower has entertained at children's birthday parties, company picnics, and restaurants. You will learn many of her clowning techniques in this book. I strongly urge you to purchase this book, study it, be serious about your clowning, and soon you will be a part of our clowning fraternity. Clowning can be fun but please stay away from squirting flowers.

John Kennedy, Magician

I have been a close-up magician and magic inventor my entire life. I currently own and operate John Kennedy Magic where I design and manufacture magic for magicians around the world.

I met Leslie in the 1980s in the Washington D.C. area where I collaborated with top close-up and sleight-of-hand magicians. Leslie was clowning at the time but also had an intense interest in magic. She somehow managed to charm herself into our elite magic group. She was fiercely determined to learn the latest and most advanced sleight-of-hand moves and routines.

At the same time, she was mentoring with top stage magicians and learning their craft. All this while learning clowning from the top in that field.

Leslie is uniquely qualified to bring together magic and clowning like few other people on the planet. Her book is a treasure trove of practical routines, handlings, and advice for the serious magic clown hobbyist and professional. I highly recommended it.

Introduction

Leslie Ann Akin as Flower T. Clown in 1983

Are you a clown who performs at birthday parties, picnics, parades or visits hospitals? Do you try to overcome the fear of performing and creating a show worth paying for? Are you clueless about how to start?

This book is for clowns or wannabe clowns who already have their makeup and wardrobe established. There is a lot of good content available on those subjects. I decided not to be redundant.

You will learn how to start a gag file for your one-liners, plan birthday party routines, work a company picnic, meet hospital staff and patients and a lot more.

I started out as a town clown during the mid-'70s when women clowns were uncommon and circus clowns were thought of as the elite clowns, having reached the pinnacle of success under the Big Top. Town clowns idolized circus clowns as the true professionals.

When I joined a short circus tour I was beyond over the moon thrilled. I trained for five months, four hours each day, juggling and learning that comic timing is everything, unless you're eager to be on the wrong side of a swinging broom.

I thought, "Now I'll be a real clown, a circus clown!" The skills I learned training for the circus tour and the tour itself changed my perspective about clowning. I proved to myself that I could do it. Yet after accomplishing that monumental undertaking, I realized I didn't have to be a circus clown to be a great clown. I could have learned most of the skills with the help of other local professionals. Like Dorothy from *The Wizard of Oz,* I discovered I didn't have to leave home to find what was already inside me and within my reach.

I've experienced everything in the clown world one could—parties, picnics, parades, circuses, even The White House. My 15 years of clowning and writing for *Laugh-Makers Magazine* was a joy. Those articles were a splendid start for this book. I mistakenly thought it would be a breeze to pull this book together, edit the columns and go to print. Holy Bat-clown, it took months. I agonized over every word, I rewrote, added new content, and under duress from my publisher, wrapped it up.

What's to follow? Tips, facts, and stories—all first-hand experiences learned from walking many miles in those oversized shoes.

Now, on to chapter one.

Contents

"You can't use up creativity. The more you use it, the more you have."

—Maya Angelou

Chapter 1
Wacky One-liners

Comedy interview material and a collection of funny lines you are sure will work, are a big help in audience participation shows. They give you confidence, help you establish rapport more quickly and allow you to make smoother transitions between routines.

Your Gag File

In my early days of clowning, the mid-'70s, I created a gag file. I had not developed my entire comedy magic show and relied on physical comedy, and refined silliness to a high art. I added something new until the show came together, even if it was only a one-liner. (Read the Tray Table Routine in Chapter 7.)

Back to the gag file. I researched riddles, jokes, and humorous stories. When the time was right I could turn those jokes around, making them appear spontaneous. People who hired me often said I had the gift of gab. They didn't need to know I put my gag file to great use.

Here's an example of using a riddle that always played beautifully. When I was balloon making a parent often stood nearby. When I saw a dad with an alligator on his polo shirt, I said, "Dad, I see you have an alligator on your shirt. What do you get when you cross an alligator with a skunk?" Dad didn't know but was curious for the answer. "A pair of shoes nobody will wear . . . except me!" Everyone laughed. I added "except me" to the riddle.

I recommend developing a gag file that you can refer to before you perform walk-arounds, meet and greet or shows. A gag file can help you develop a strong clown persona, especially if you deliver it in full-on character.

Your Stage or Party Show

Your first volunteer, even if eager to be onstage, doesn't know exactly what to expect. They will often have that glazed-over look in their eyes—you would too if you were six years old and everyone was staring.

To relieve anticipation, I begin an interview with the child by asking questions, like "What's your name?" and "What do you do for a living?" Most of the time, the response is

"I go to school." My reply is, "Oh a professional kid, huh?" Often the kids will shake their head Yes or reply, "Yes" and that always gets a laugh from the audience.

Then I usually say, "Smile! You're in show business" or "Smile, it's in the contract!" I help the volunteer by gently pushing the corners of their mouth up. Better yet is when the child reacts to Smile with a pasted-on, toothy grin. The audience always laughs.

This sort of patter, used before leaping into a magic trick or routine work well for me, and I know the audience will always respond because they have so many times before. On another level, I think that this sort of getting-to-know-you interview tells the audience to relax, because we're going to have some fun.

When I perform at schools, I enjoy using the assistance of an adult for a portion of my show. It's not always easy to get an adult to volunteer to assist a clown.

I ask, "Who would like to volunteer . . . (pause) their teacher?" Children's hands are already waving vigorously as they yell, "Pick me!" The children will always continue waving and yelling to volunteer their teacher. Teachers will laugh and try their best to look invisible. I'll ask one child, "I see you want to volunteer your teacher!" By that time, it's clear who the teacher is. Then I ask the audience to give a big round of applause, for the volunteer! This is a wonderful way to gently and clowningly get an adult onstage with you.

During a birthday party, I use the same technique but adapt it for this close-up style of performance. I look directly into the eyes of the birthday child and ask, "Is there anyone here who would like to volunteer . . . (pause, for all the yelling and waving) their father?!" The birthday child always says yes. Then I announce, "Well, dad, it looks like you're the lucky volunteer!" And in classic Price Is Right style, I yell, "Come on down!" Take note: Not every birthday child has their father at the show. Adapt this technique of selecting an adult volunteer, only after you are sure of who the adults are at the party.

Children having the opportunity to see their parents or any authority figure do something silly is a treat for them, as well as those present.

The parents are blindsided by the request to involve them in the show, and ultimately delighted. This is a true Kodak moment, as lots of photos are taken during this portion of the show.

After the fun of having an audience volunteer, ask the audience to give them a big round of applesauce-er, uh, applause—before your volunteer leaves the stage. I make it a point to thank each of them for being a terrific magical clown assistant and give a magical clown assistant certificate for each volunteer—and the adults love receiving a certificate as much as the kids.

I place their name on it, and sign it—everything except notarize it. When I meet some of these folks at other shows again, they have told me that they have their magical clown assistant certificate framed and hanging proudly in their office, along with their other university diplomas. Gotta love that!

You will get the timing and sensitivity fine-tuned as you use one-liners and bits like this over and over again.

"It's getting harder and harder to differentiate between schizophrenics and people talking on a cell phone. It still brings me up short to walk by somebody who appears to be talking to themselves."

—Bob Newhart

Chapter 2
Ring-A-Ding-Ding

We'll explore the comedic value of telephone routines. First, we'll talk about the props you will need. I recommend using a receiver and cord from a toy phone or better yet, a genuine telephone receiver and cord. I found that an old-fashioned phone receiver is effective. People do a dou-ble-take and aren't at all sure it isn't a real call. This momen-tary uncertainty helps them suspend disbelief and enter into playfulness.

A second prop, called the phoney ring, is a box with a push button. Each time you push the button, you'll hear a single ring that sounds like a telephone. You control the length and number of rings. Attach the cord of the receiver with a safety pin to the inside of your pocket or prop bag. Conceal both the receiver and the phoney ring box inside your pocket. The element of surprise is great when you pull a phone out of your pocket!

Let's begin with how to use the phone when you're interacting with an audience where people don't know one another. Sometimes I'll ring the phone, answer it, and hand it to someone saying, "It's for you." The usual reply is—but there's no one there! As I take the phone back, I'll comment "You're kidding!" I listen a moment and say "Well sure, he's right here." Then I'll carry on a short conversation. Soon I'll ask the caller to hold for a moment, put my hand over the mouthpiece and turn to the person who said no one was there. I'll say, "They're speaking in sign language. I'll interpret so hold on a moment." I resume the phone conversation. The audience ends up with a she's got to be kidding look on their faces and burst out laughing.

Tune in to Your Audience

The real value in the telephone humor is the opportunity to gear your humor to individuals you meet. Everyone, no matter what age, profession or way of life, basks in personal attention. You can make these bits more personal by gauging them to the age group you're interacting with. A phone call to an eight-year-old might be from Kermit the Frog. The call you set up for a business person could be from their stockbroker. Establish common ground by including famous personalities into your phone routines.

I ring the hidden phoney ring box, pull the phone out of my pocket and answer it. I listen for a second and wave the phone in mid-air as I say "It's your stockbroker, E.F. Hutton! Everybody listen!" I hand the phone to the person who is business-like, stand back and announce that the call is long distance. Another way to play this gag, is to move in a little closer and say it's a close call. When I get the phone back, I talk with E.F. Hutton. I listen for a moment and say, "Okay, E.F., I'll tell him . . . Bye . . . No! I didn't mean BUY, I meant goodbye!" That last line always gets a laugh if you remember to act very surprised at being misunderstood.

This funny business was created when I was clowning in a restaurant, and developed over the years. I was entertaining a family with a four-year-old boy, and I knelt to get closer to the child.

He was enjoying the visit, and I rang my phoney ring box. Since I was kneeling, my pockets weren't very accessible. The boy was sitting in a booth with his feet dangling. The next thing I knew, I was talking into his foot saying, "Hello? Yes, he's here. It's for you!" The boy giggled and smiled in disbelief. He hesitated for a moment, then said, "Hello" into his own shoe. He believed in the magic and fantasy for that moment. Now, when I pull this same phone and foot and foot gag and a child says, "I can't hear anything," I usually say, "That's funny, let me check." I then hold their shoe and speak into the sole, using some of the following one liners:

"Oh, I see, Miss Piggy. Kermit the Frog has a people in his throat?!"

There's a lot of sole in this conversation.

"You're not a heel, are you?"

"You've jogged my memory."

"Are you sure my friend just stepped out?"

(Laced shoes) "We're a little tied up right now."

(Sneakers) "Do you sneak into the cookie jar?"

(Loafers) :Do you loaf around much?"

By this time, you will have received comments, chuckles and groans from the adults in your audience. You can always quip, "No stepping on my lines, please." Remember, a groan is always as good as a laugh. Playing the old Maxwell Smart, Agent 99, talking into your shoe, could be funny if you think your audience will respond to it. You'll discover more one liners as you get into this gag, or you'll find a better way to use the ones I have listed.

One of the best ways to establish common ground is to build famous personalities or characters into your phone routines.

When I greet a senior citizen, I'll ring the phone, answer it and say "Well, she's right here, hold on." As I hand the person the phone, I tell her "It's B.G., and that's not the Brothers Gibb!" Seniors will know you're referring to Benny Goodman. They'll enjoy that you recalled their heyday. When I get the phone back, I'll listen and say, "Oh, B.G., that's wonderful. You're stomping at the Savoy with Ella (Fitzgerald). You're holding tickets? Ok, hold on a moment, you want me to give them the phone number?" I turn to my audience, saying, "B.G. asked if you can remember this number." By this time, I'm tapping my foot and snapping fingers and go into "Pennsylvania 6-5-oh-oh-oh!" Someone often says I'm too young to remember the Big Band era, so I'll comment, "I'm well preserved."

Ask yourself, will this person enjoy this humor? If your audience doesn't get it, or has no interest in your subject, that's almost the same as being offensive. You can't always be sure of what will work, but you can be sensitive to people.

*"Comedy is based on truth. You take the truth
and you add a little curlicue at the end."*

—Sid Caesar

Chapter 3
Tiny Knee-slappers

Let's build a few small props that cost little in terms of time and dollars, yet play big. These props play well for outdoor promotions, picnics, parades, and meet-and-greet clowning.

The WANDerful Broom, Little Mac, the Burger Whisperer and the Oversized Clown Thermometer were all designed by professional clowns who specialize in close-up clowning. They built them with small carrying space and mobility in mind. You can fit them in big pockets or in a shoulder bag for props, and you can take them anywhere.

Sometimes the written description of a prop doesn't sound like much. However, all three props yield sure-fire laughs.

WANDerful Broom

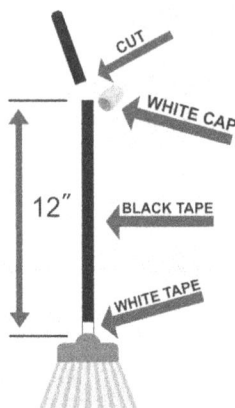

WANDerful Broom

The idea for this prop came to Danson Hanson (who clowned with the Beatty Circus) after seeing Daren Dundee's WANDerful Mop.

Dan liked the mop, and it seemed perfect for stage shows, but he wanted to condense the size for birthday party shows, plus develop a routine that would fit his clown character.

Construction

Start with a child-size broom, which you can find in a toy store. Saw off a piece to get it down to the 16-inch size that fits well in pockets or prop bags. Wrap the handle in black tape. Place a strip of white tape at the end of the handle near the bristles and place a white furniture cap on the end of the broom handle for the magical finishing touch.

This is a snappy alternative to the feather dusters every clown uses. It's also easy to balance on the palm of your hand or on your chin. If you drop a juggling prop, you could grab the broom to replace or sweep away the fallen object. Then add the broom to your juggling patter and say you needed a little magic to clean up your act.

After producing confetti in your act, someone in the audience may ask who will clean up the mess. If not, appoint a volunteer to assist you. Explain you have a magic wand that will do the job. Expose only the wand section, not the bristles, from behind your magic stand or out of your prop bag or pocket. Explain the amazing powers this wand possesses and that it will clean up all the confetti.

Ask the volunteer to help you, and as the child steps forward, expose the entire WAND while placing it in their hands. Place your hands on the wand along with the child's and show a sweeping motion while saying "Just wave it like this!"

Oversized Thermometer

This version of the clown thermometer is by Danson Hanson.

Construction

You will need:

- One clear plastic shower rod cover cut into an 18-inch piece for each thermometer
- White poster board cut into a three-fourths-inch by seventeen-inch piece
- Two five-eighths-inch rubber furniture caps painted with chrome paint
- Black and red markers.

Draw on both sides of the poster board to simulate the inside of a thermometer. Finish it with the black and red markers. Place the decorated poster board inside the clear plastic tube and cap both ends with the chrome furniture caps. It's as simple as that!

When visiting people in hospitals, I introduce myself, and as I explain that I take their temperature, I show the over-sized thermometer. The patients always laugh and say you're not sticking that thing in my mouth! I respond with OK, bend over! Talk about comic relief! The staff gets a BIG chuckle out of this prop, too.

In shows, you can use the oversized thermometer to check the temperature of an assistant in the audience. Ask them to say "Ah," then place the thermometer under their arm. If you use a dove pan in a magic act, you can use the thermometer to check the temperature of the pan before producing something, and then use it as a magic wand.

You can make three thermometers from one shower rod tube. The material cost is low, and it will only take about 15 minutes to construct.

Little Mac, the Burger Whisperer

Here's a fantastic puppet prop from Daren Dundee, a world-class prop master.

I have used this Little Mac to help me select a child from the audience to take part in the show. Little Mac, the Burger Whisperer whispers in my ear and the performer relays the message to the audience. Choosing an assistant becomes part of the show in an amusing way. This puppet is open to a clowns' favorite brand of humor, puns. Trying to ketchup, not cutting the mustard, and relishing the idea are just a few campy comments you can use.

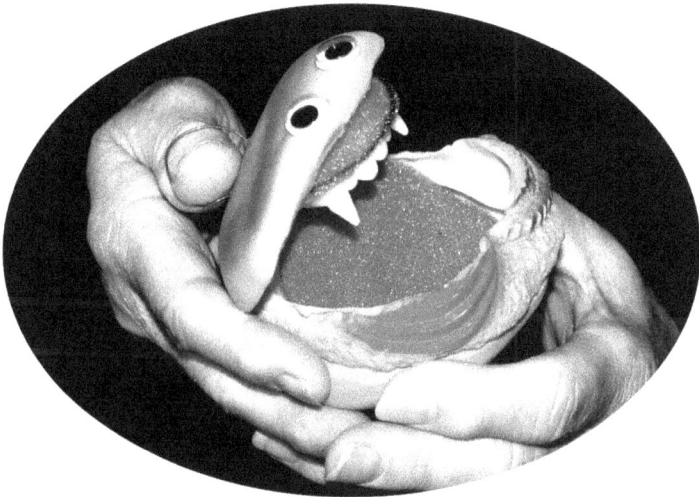

Purchase a rubber dog toy that looks like a hamburger. Most pet departments carry these and some have a squeaker inside.

Start by slicing the burger from one side to the other, leaving two inches attached at the back. Glue a pair of googly eyes onto the burger bun.

Poke two small holes on the top and on the bottom with soft floral wire through the holes, twist it together on the inside, forming an outside loop.

Your thumb goes through the top loop and your middle finger goes through the bottom loop to manipulate Little Mac's mouth.

Just as Danson Hanson built on Daren Dundee's idea, you'll discover props and routines that fit your character. Remember, it's not the prop that is funny all by itself. It's your uncommon spin on the routine that sets you apart.

*"Life's like a movie, write your own ending.
Keep believing, keep pretending."*

— Jim Henson

Chapter 4
Colossal Knee-slappers

Big Wheel, or the Invisible Bus, Taxi, or Limo

The Big Wheel has proven to be one of my most useful and powerful walk-arounds. It is simple and the comedic potential is huge.

Construction

You will need:

- A child-sized hula hoop (large hula hoops make for tired arms)
- Colored plastic tape
- A bike horn
- An optional side mirror

Wrap the tape around the wheel. Next, stretch a piece of tape across the center of the hoop to simulate the center of a real steering wheel. Stretch another piece of tape along the back of the first piece so you won't have any sticky places. Add the cross piece of tape and be sure to back that one too. If you prefer, you can make a "Y" instead of a cross in the hoop. Wrap the bike horn into the center with plastic tape. Attach the side mirror to see where you have been.

I'm sure you will discover many uses for this prop. Let me share with you some of my favorites. When rounding up children to play games or to see your show, just ask them to climb onto your bus, and before you know it, you'll have the children following you Pied Piper style. You can encourage the children to mime the actions of getting into and riding the bus. There's a lot of room for play.

At a Christmas show, I led 60 children with the Big Wheel over to the tree they would be decorating. We rode the invisible bus as we laughed and sang carols. The adults were stirred with emotion as we approached them. This was one of the moments of clowning that touched my heart.

I performed with a circus clown at a school show. When it came time for him to unicycle, he used my Big Wheel as his steering wheel. This made unicycling even funnier.

The Big Wheel is a great entrance prop, for a group of clowns doing a show together, or for solo shows you perform at people's homes or anywhere. Whenever I entertain where parking is a problem, I enter and say, "I had to bring the car inside, there aren't any parking spaces out there! Did you know I get 50 smiles to the gallon?"

The Big Wheel is a knockout for car promotions. Comments from sales people are priceless. The straighter I play it, the funnier it gets. They're laughing and I can't understand why. When salespeople inquire, "Where's the engine?" I respond, "This is it, this is my car. My trendy new car doesn't need gas or electric to run. And I have the manual!"

Big Wheel funny-business you can use.

- Your Uber driver is here.
- Climb in the back seat, strap on your seatbelt.
- Roll the windows up. The air conditioner is on.
- I worked to buy this car, so I could go to work. It cost a whole $3.95.
- I love having a car no one wants to steal.
- I chose the road less traveled. Now look where I am.
- I decided to go green in a big way.
- I need some help pushing this car to the gas station. I have a flat tire.

- I pick up hitchhikers. I tell frogs to hop in.
- I never get parking tickets, because I removed the windshield wipers.
- It's a compact. There's not much under the hood. (wink)
- Why does a chicken coop have 2 doors? Because with 4 doors it would be a chicken sedan.
- How do fleas travel from place to place? By itch-hiking.
- Knock knock! Who's there? Cargo! Cargo who? Car go better if we fill it with gas.
- Knock, knock! Who's there? Colin. Colin who? Colin all cars!Colin all cars!
- Knock, knock! Who's there? Wanda. Wanda who? Wanda where I put my car keys!

Clown at WURK

Clown at WURK is a silly sight gag when you're booked to clown for several hours. A lull in customer traffic allows this gag to play well. You'll be doing something funny as customers approach or pass by.

Lie down on a bench, sidewalk, or the grass by the establishment or place you're clowning for and pretend to be asleep. Exaggerated snoring, adding wiggles, tossing and turning add to the visual effect. All the while, the Clown at WURK sign is where everyone can see it and me together.

Passers-by always chuckle. Children will stand at your side and say, "That's not how you spell work!" I'll open one eye and answer, "Well, how do you spell it? W-E-R-K or W-I-R-K?" You can also play this gag with the oversized sunglasses and a large umbrella and get good laughs. Lie there exclaiming, "I love my WURK!" Children will clarify you're not working.

Play this gag for about 5 minutes. Much longer and you'd be lying down on the job. This is a good bit for almost any style clown, and tailor-made for the tramp clown. Covering up with a Wall Street Journal completes the picture. Clown at WURK is reminiscent of the Depression era and comic relief for today.

This gag is perfect for a parade routine. I've done Clown at WURK on a rolling flatbed with another clown pulling it, while I sport my oversized shades, waving to the crowd. We traded places mid-parade to share the hardest part of the routine, pulling the flatbed.

Assembly of Clown at WURK

1. Cut 2 pieces of thin wood or particle board (28 inches wide by 20 inches high). This size is large enough to play big small enough to carry.

2. Attach the two pieces with hinges at the top.

3. Decorate, paint, and trim. I suggest bright colors like bright red and yellow. Trim the edges with colored tape or paint.

"Comedy is based upon very old principles of which I can readily name seven. They are, in short: the joke, exaggeration, ridicule, ignorance, surprise, the pun, and finally, the comic situation."

— Jack Benny

Chapter 5
Whopping Warm-ups

Remember when theatres showed Tom and Jerry cartoons before the feature film? Remember the last time you went to the circus? If you arrived 20 minutes early, you saw clowns in the ring doing come-in. They were getting the audience's attention, firing them up for the main event.

Whether your warm-up is for another performer's show (after all, clowns are tailor-made creatures for attracting attention and getting laughs!) or for your own show, it is a crucial element that makes a difference in how the audience will respond throughout the rest of the performance.

Warm-ups prepare the audience to focus and realize It's Showtime! They set the stage for the audience to begin laughing, clapping, participating and they give the audience a chance to take you in. This is their introduction to your character.

At picnics, fairs, and malls, your warm-up may be one of the ways you draw a crowd for your show. These warm-ups should be highly visual and dynamic. Simplicity and audience participation are the main ingredients of good warm-ups for clown shows.

My warm-ups are usually three to five minutes long, sometimes shorter. Following are a few ideas from my experiences.

Simple-Silly-Slapstick Tray Table Routine

This is a routine superb for beginner clowns and experienced performers. The routine evolves, getting better as you gain experience and learn more about physical comedy. I developed this bit of baffling buffoonery during my early days of clowning in 1976 and it always brought gobs of laughs.

This is a classic, silly physical comedy bit. You will get several minutes of razzle-dazzle from this warm-up.

You'll need a metal TV tray table. You can find them at yard sales or second-hand stores. The base and legs fold and are separate from the tray.

Here's the comedic set-up, the way I performed it at birthday parties before I purchased my suitcase table. Enter carrying your prop bag and the unassembled tray table. Introduce yourself and greet the birthday child, expressing how thrilled you are to be there for their special day.

"Are you ready for the show? I'll get this table ready." Can you see it coming? I set my prop bag and tray top off to the side and hold up the legs/frame. After looking it over I step into the floppy frame and get caught in it. I'll walk a few steps forward, then backward, looking perplexed. By this time, the children enjoy telling me I'm doing it wrong.

I step out of the frame, look at it, then place it over my head, again walking back and forth. Then I notice the tray top, put that on my head while the frame is on my shoulders. All the while, the children are trying to direct the bumbling clown.

I fumble as I figure out how to make the tray fit into the frame. Eventually, I get the tray clamped to the frame, but it's attached to the wrong part, upside down. It looks funny to see the tray flying off to the side.

This funny business continues even after I've got the tray put together, but it's still upside down, tray facing the floor. "We did it!" Again the children direct me as I bumble through setting the tray up.

Now it's time to ask the birthday child to come forward to set the tray table into the right position. They get to be the star and earn applause for being an outstanding assistant.

Now you can drape the tray with festive fabric and use it for props during your show.

This routine is inexpensive, lightweight and easy to tote. Entering as your clown character with a tray table and setting it up as if you were not a clown, would not be funny.

When you're in true clown character, you're setting up your show while inspiring snickers and silliness through predicaments you find yourself in.

A Teaser

When I performed school shows I poked my head from behind the curtain just before the show. The children giggled and squealed with delight. This was just a teaser, short and funny, and got the audience fired up, anticipating what would happen next.

Use Your Other Talents

Whatever the main part of your show is, you may want to try using a talent other than your specialty for your audience warm-up. I've learned this makes my act more versatile and offers me great opportunities for developing new material.

For example, I used my skills as a juggler to warm up the audience before my comedy magic show with up-tempo circus music in the background. It's a great way to test audience reaction to new material without depending on it to carry the whole show. I even added a few hat tricks to my warm-up. Positive audience response inspired me to learn more circus arts skills.

Young Children

Instead of using your usual warm-up for children under five years old, you may want to use a friendly looking soft puppet, a spring animal or some sponge magic and work closely with the children. They will get used to you and you can discover and deal with any frightened ones right off the bat.

Magic Word Warm-up

If you haven't used a warm-up previously, here's a simple but very effective one you might try. Ask the children to shout out a magic word together. At the end of the school year, my popular magic words are Summer Vacation! At a picnic, you might use the name of the sponsor or company. My all-time favorite magic words are Cadabra-Abra!

Good clownies do takes in threes, so directing the children to say the words three times, each time yelling louder, can create a lot of energy. On the third try, you could magically produce something, like spring flowers as the magic words are shouted.

This is a visual climax to the children's loudest attempt at shouting the magic words. Instead of doing magic, you might want to take a fall and ooze right into a backward roll as if the children had shouted you into doing it.

What you decide to practice and perform for your warm-ups is limited only by your imagination. You could probably do two or three minutes of hysterical physical comedy just by trying to take off your gloves, coat or hat.

Or you could learn to throw a few spiffy hat spins and tricks, use puppetry or ventriloquism, juggle, or spin a plate.

Whatever you choose, remember warm-ups will make a difference in the success of your shows. Don't leave out this time-tested technique.

"The only limit to your impact is your imagination and commitment."

— Tony Robbins

Chapter 6
Nitty-Gritty of Birthday Parties

Over the years I have met performers, whose opinion of children's parties is that they're easy—a piece of birthday cake, so to speak. Some have even told me they don't have prepared material. They wing it. It's just a party for little kids, right? Ha! Nothing is farther from the truth.

To perform children's shows, you must like, understand and respect children and see them as a viable audience. They're not just little kids you can trick into thinking you're a real entertainer. Children are honest, tune into an insincere performer, and can tell when you're not prepared. Children will pick up on these vibrations and they'll call you out.

The birthday child is the guest of honor and the parents expect this celebration to be a highlight of their year. You are invited because you will make this celebration memorable and loads of fun.

Fine and dandy, you say, but how can I get beyond just showing up, pulling out the props I've got, and hoping my character will pull it off?

Here are some tips and techniques I've learned during my fifteen years on the birthday party circuit. The most valuable piece of advice offered came from a professional magician several years ago. He told me that my sense of presence, confidence, and control over children's behavior would improve if I concentrated on developing and performing one well-planned show. I doubted this at first. I thought doing the same show over and over would stifle my spontaneity and creativity. He was a successful magician—and who can argue with success? So, I gave it a try.

After performing one comedy magic show I developed for all my party bookings for several months, I had to admit he was right. My timing, pacing, delivery, handling of props and sense of presence improved a great deal. I sensed this change in the audience response and the feedback from parents. Often hosts mentioned that I held their attention and the entire family enjoyed the show.

I became comfortable with the show and felt a wonderful sense of freedom and fun about it. Because I knew the mechanics of my routines and structure so well, I could enjoy the audience even more and engage them in more interaction and comedy by-play.

The show seems spontaneous, and it is a foundation which I build on. I don't have to reinvent the wheel for each appearance, yet I can add new bits to the foundation as I discover and develop them.

A prepared show like this will also help you survive those rare parties where you're faced with an audience that sits back as if you were on TV or hesitates to take part. You'll be performing a tight show and, even without the greatest audience response, you'll still shine.

For repeat bookings or those where you're booked in the same neighborhood more than a few times, you may wish to put together a second show, Party Show B. This will help ease the possibilities of a child blurting out the surprise ending before you get to it and the I-saw-that-before remarks.

Some busy performers on the birthday circuit pack two complete shows, each in a different traveling case. If time is close between parties on the same day, they can arrive at the second party, pull out Party Show B and not worry about resetting the first show. Try it. It works.

Here are a few more birthday party tips:

1. **Set-Up Time:** When booking a party, I always inform the parents I will need five minutes of set-up time in the room where the show will be, without the kids present. Most of my props are pre-loaded, but there are a few which must be set up on the scene. The children enter what is now my space. This technique seems to generate a sense of show time and the bonus is better behavior.

2. **Suitcase Table:** I've found that working from a suitcase table is practical for me. I can hide props, gimmicks, puppets, wands behind the table; they're in reach and can be on top of the table as I need them, yet the kids can't grab anything or see what's coming next. The table lends a showmanship atmosphere and cuts down on searching for props. It brings order instead of working from a jumbled prop bag. At the end of the show, I pack props in the bottom, fold down the top portion, and wheel the table to my vehicle. It's neat, simple, saves time and worth the investment.

3. **Content:** The birthday child is the star of the show and should be singled out if they're eager to take part in the show. Make the party content something the children can relate to. Stories and patter referring to their current heroes or cartoon characters have strong appeal among young audiences. You won't want all your patter to revolve around popular heroes or cartoon characters, but including something topical always goes a long way in kids' shows. Kids also relate to food and

eating, video games and current TV shows. Routines revolving around this subject always seem to work. Include one of the adults in your show for lots of laughs.

4. **Invest:** Invest not only time, but also money in your show. Your clown character sells you and your show. Hosts like to see what they're paying. When I invested in magic, props and improved my wardrobe, the response from clients led to more referrals. Razzle-dazzle never hurt anyone's show.

If you're on the birthday party circuit, you're entertaining one of the most difficult and demanding audiences—children and their parents. My personal favorites are four generations in one room. There is something in the show for everyone. I'm a fan of Rocky and Bullwinkle and loved the puns and one-liners tossed in for the adults to understand more than the kids.

Sponge Bob is another popular cartoon character kids love There's humor for the adults as well. Using this character, you can play off the wisecracking to keep your show topical.

It feels wonderful to leave a show with children to great grandparents smiling and saying how much they loved the show.

Develop one solid show using your special talents you'll be proud to offer. Practice your routines until you've got them right, and your timing and anticipation of audience response will become so sharp you can include even more impromptu comedy.

*"Courage is being scared to death but
saddling up anyway."*

— John Wayne

Chapter 7
Mirthdays Are for Laughing

Mirthdays, birthdays, whatever you like to call these celebrations, they're always a highlight for the children and prime territory for Kodak moments.

When I decided to give birthday parties a try it was 1976. This was long before clowns at parties became the norm. I started small, offering a 30-minute visit with the children, entering with a tray table (Chapter 5) and getting loads of laughs and interaction from the kids telling me how to set it up. I performed some easy-to-carry pocket magic, such as Mr. Party Animal (Chapter 9). We sang songs and I created balloon sculptures for the kids and started developing amusing bits to do with each sculpture.

One of my all-time favorite one-liners was to stretch the balloons and ask, "Did you know these balloons are summer balloons?" The kids said no. I responded, "Yes, these are summer balloons (while stretching them). Summer red and summer green."

But I digress. Once I became comfortable with parties and felt more confident doing them, I became fascinated with magic. I knew if I was going to pursue the art of prestidigitation I would need a mentor or two. I joined magic clubs, and went to every magic show I could. I realized I loved magic when the presenter was funny. So that's when I decided to become a magic clown.

Over time I developed a solid comedy magic show. I wanted to create stories that required interaction from the kids. The magic was a medium of charming visuals that made the stories more entertaining.

In the next four chapters, you'll learn my favorite magic tricks for birthday parties. And I kid you not, these effects have very little to do with slight-of-hand skills. The most challenging part of the performance is performing them in your authentic clown character and bringing your special something to the party.

Get ready to make 'em laugh.

"It is better to fail in originality than to succeed in imitation."

— Herman Melville

Chapter 8
Hanky Panky! Where's My Hanky?!

Silkola is a standard magic prop you can purchase from most magic dealers locally or online. The effect itself comprises of placing a circular can over an empty soda bottle. A silk is vanished. Next, when the can is lifted, the vanished silk is found inside the soda bottle.

I've developed a routine for this effect, which I use to open all my clown/magic shows. I use the Silkola and another standard magic prop (Popcorn Dye Box) to vanish the silk. I call the silk a hanky in kids' shows.

Silkola comes with a bottle cap, which I omit from the trick. It is just my personal choice not to use it, and I still get strong audience response without using it. It's up to you.

It's time I shared my Star Wars Silkola routine with you because it's really favorite with my audiences. Let's get started!

I ask the audience if they like movies. Of course, their response is positive. Do you like *Star Wars, Return of the Jedi,* or *The Last Jedi?*

I wonder if I can get a young man to volunteer for this Star Wars magic trick? (I choose a boy who is eager but one who appears to follow directions easily.)

Well, what is your name? Jimmy? Well Jimmy, have you ever been in show business before? No? Well Jimmy, when you're in show business, you have to smile at the audience. It's in the contract! (Jimmy gives a big toothy grin to the audience. Big yuks from the audience.)

Jimmy, I'd like you to pretend something for me. Say Yes! (Jimmy says yes). Jimmy, I'd like you to pretend you are (giggle, giggle) Luke (giggle, giggle) Sillywalker! (Jimmy and everyone else will laugh.)

Luke Sillywalker, I would like to ask you what you like to drink when you go to the movies. (I partially cover my mouth, and in a loud stage whisper, ask Luke Sillywalker to say "Coke!" Luke Sillywalker says "Coke." (More yuks.)

Now Luke Sillywalker, watch carefully. I am going to put this soda bottle inside this cylinder. Say yes. (Luke says yes). Now Luke Sillywalker, I would like you to keep one eye here, one eye there (point to the audience) and one eye here (point to yourself). Okay? Jimmy will say okay. More yucks. Meanwhile, the cylinder has been placed on the magic stand.

Now I need a young lady to help with this magic trick. After choosing and interviewing the girl, I ask her to pretend that she is (giggle, giggle) Princess (giggle, giggle) Gertrude!

Princess Gertrude, I would like to know what you like to eat when you go to the movies. (I ask this as I place the popcorn box directly in her view) Again, in a loud stage whisper, I direct the volunteer, only this time I want her to say "Popcorn." Princess Gertrude will say popcorn.

Now, look inside the popcorn box, Princess Gertrude. Is there anything inside of it? (In a stage whisper, direct her to say "No!" Princess Gertrude says "No."

Now Princess Gertrude, I am going to take the hanky I used when I saw Star Wars, and put it inside the popcorn box. Say Okay! (Princess Gertrude says "Okay." I place the hanky in the popcorn box, this is how I am vanishing the silk that will eventually show up in the soda bottle.)

Princess Gertrude, could you place one arm out there (I position her left arm out into space) and put one foot out, and one arm out here. It makes the show look bigger (pause for yuks) try to make like Vanna White, that really makes the show look bigger! (more yuks).

Princess Gertrude, please take this magic wand and wave it over the popcorn box (I use the breakaway wand and go for three times. The third time I try it, I'll say May the force be with Princess Gertrude this time!

Princess Gertrude, please reach inside the popcorn box and get the hanky. (P.G. reaches inside and pops the popcorn box open by pushing through to the bottom of the box. You can help that happen by pulling up on the box. I don't notice the box is empty right away. I let the audience react to the fact that the hanky has vanished. They tell me to look, I finally look and of course, I ask Princess Gertrude where she put the hanky!)

Princess Gertrude, where did you put my hanky? P.G. will say she doesn't know what happened to it. I usually check her ears, maybe the ribbons in her hair, and even her socks. (More yuks!) Then there is the realization that comes to Flower. I usually face the audience with an enlightened look on my face. Then I turn to Luke.

Luke Sillywalker, did you have anything to do with this?! (He will deny everything. I look out at the audience.)

Well, how many of you out there say Luke Sillywalker kept one eye here (on the cylinder), one eye there (on the audience) and one eye here (on me)? There is always a difference of opinion. More yuks. Luke Sillywalker will continue to deny any responsibility for the predicament.

Let's all say the magic words! (At that, I lift the cylinder to reveal the silk inside the soda bottle).

How did you do that? I demand to know from Luke Silly-walker. Luke usually says he doesn't know. I look at the audience and just say he doesn't want to tell. That's okay, because real magicians never tell their secrets!

Then I bring Luke Sillywalker and Princess Gertrude to the front of the stage and I ask them Do you know what we're going to do?

As I place their hands together, I say (you saw it coming) I now pronounce you .... Oh! We won't do that part! (More yuks!) Well, really, we are going to take a bow. And you know what everyone else is going to do? They're going to applaud loudly!

And we do. And they do. This routine is a terrific opener for a magic show, and you can take this movie format and adapt it to fit any popular movie.

*"Comedy is based on truth. You take the truth
and you add a little curlicue at the end."*

— Sid Caesar

Chapter 9
Mr. Party Animal

Let's look at how two magic props, the Sponge Ball to Bunny
and a Mouth Coil, can come to life in shows for younger
children. I performed these tricks at birthday parties, stage
shows and during walk-arounds for years with superb audience response. This routine works well in the middle of a
show because you will have time to assess who the giggler
is in the audience.

Part 1

Ask the audience, "Have you seen my little friend around?
His name is Mr. Party Animal, and sometimes he hides from
me. Sometimes he hides in ears! Can you check your ears
and see if he's in there?"

Kids in the audience will check their ears.

"He likes to hide in pockets and sleeves, especially if you have peanut butter and banana sandwiches in your pockets and sleeves."Kids will check their pockets and sleeves.

"Mr. Party Animal likes to hide in shoes and socks, especially if you have nachos in your shoes and socks! Do you?"

Kids check their shoes and socks. If you wear oversized clown shoes, this is a great time to draw attention to them by checking them out looking for the stray creature.

Repeat, "Has anyone seen Mr. Party Animal?" Direct the question to one child you will use as your volunteer.

Note: I chose a girl about four or five years old, who showed signs of being an easy giggler.

Select your volunteer to help find Mr. Party Animal. After the usual interview, I ask permission before I check in their ear. They always say yes because you've built their trust by taking it slow and giving them a choice.

Look in the volunteer's ear, respond by being very surprised, and tell the audience "There's something in there!"

Look again, show surprise, and giggle. Then, by palming the Sponge Ball-to-Bunny, produce it, still in the shape of a ball, from your volunteer's ear exclaiming, "It's Mr. Party Animal! How did you get him in your ear?"

The sponge ball is in your right hand, the volunteer is on your left. Hold Mr. Party Animal (still just a sponge ball) close enough to your ear to make it appear as if the ball is saying something. Give it some movement so this has a chance of looking lifelike.

Respond by saying (as you look at the sponge ball), "You want to eat what? A carrot?"

Giggle, look away from the sponge ball and ask the volunteer, "Why would Mr. Party Animal ever want to eat a carrot? Silly, isn't it!" As you ask, roll the ball in your right hand so it becomes the sponge bunny.

Continue to look toward your volunteer. The volunteer and the audience answer the question as predicted, "Why would Mr. Party Animal want to eat a carrot?" as they point to the sponge bunny, yelling, "He's a bunny!"

Remember, the volunteer is on my left, the sponge bunny is in my right hand, and you haven't seen it as a bunny yet. When the volunteer points to the bunny, you'll gain extra comedic mileage by following your eyes down her arm all the way to the bunny. When you see the bunny, do a double take, like you're seeing it for the first time. You are just as surprised as the kids. "Wow! How did you get Mr. Party Animal to become a bunny?"

Note: This could be the end of this magic routine. I continue the trick, delivering more funny business.

Optional Part 2

Ask your volunteer, "May I check your ear one more time?"

They'll say yes. You'll check their ear and giggle as I say, "Mr. Party Animal was having a party in your ear!"

You'll palm the mouth coil near their ear and say to the volunteer, "Hey! We'd like you to be part of the party, too!" Produce the mouth coil streamer (it appears to come from the volunteer's ear), little by little, to get the most response from it. Use this opportunity to produce the mouth coil as a super visual by twirling it in the performance area.

You could end this portion of the routine by draping your volunteer in the mouth coil or continue by vanishing the mouth coil to produce one more magic effect.

Optional Part 3

Place the mouth coil in a crystal silk cylinder and produce a Happy Birthday silk or small favors for the audience. You could use a magic change bag instead of a cylinder to vanish the mouth coil and produce small favors or a beautiful silk.

Give the routine a try or create your own keeping in mind the key concept here. By giving the sponge ball a name and treating it as a real character rather than as an inanimate object, audience response will be greater.

The routine runs about five to six minutes and acts as a perfect filler without option 3. It packs small, so it's easy to carry for picnics, walk-arounds, restaurant table-hopping, and parties.

"All I really want to do is make people laugh."

— Larry Pisoni

Chapter 10
Comedy Magic with Peanuts!

Peanuts, a funny audience participation routine, is similar to a sucker trick, but following a strong blow-off, the volunteer ends up with a prize.

Props: The main prop you will use is a chick pan (available from magic dealers); small tray; real dollar bill; fake hand (non-bloody); over-sized fake dollar bills; peanuts (in the shell); clown bow tie or long tie; clown-like hat; and a clown nose or red sticker.

Set-up: Put the real dollar bill in the bottom half of the chick pan and place on the tray. Load the peanuts in the top part of the chick pan. Place the loaded compartment next to the bottom part of the chick pan on the tray. Keep the fake hand and the big dollar bill out of sight until the appropriate time.

The Routine: You will use a volunteer from the audience. To begin, ask, "Is there anyone in the audience who would like to be Clownie for the Day? I need someone who can follow directions well, and (pause) someone who would like to TRY to win a dollar!"

Show the dollar and watch those hands raise and the kids shout, "Pick me! Pick me!" I shout, "Sit down, Dad!" which gets a good laugh.

I remind the audience that the volunteer must be able to follow directions and be eager to be our star as Clownie for the day.

If I'm at a birthday party where there is a guest of honor, I rarely choose the birthday kid to assist with this trick since it is a sucker effect. In fact, I've found that choosing the right volunteer is key to success; otherwise, it will fall flat. Over the years, I've learned to spot my Peanuts! assistant early in the show. I choose a boy (sometimes girls don't enjoy being dressed as a clown) who is five to nine years old and neither too verbal nor too shy.

I bring the volunteer up, asking the audience to give him a big round of applause. Then I ask his name (let's call this kid Brian), ask if his wife is in the audience, etc. After the interview, I tell Brian, "You're Clownie for the Day, so you should look the part!"

I bring out a clown tie, show it to him, and ask permission to place the tie on him. Next, the hat goes on, along with the finishing touch, a sponge clown nose or red sticker. "Now we have our Clownie for the Day and it's time to take the clownie promise."

"Brian," I'll explain, "This is the clownie promise. Raise your right hand and repeat after me." (You raise your right hand to lead him). "I promise (Brian repeats) to never (Brian repeats) put chocolate pudding (Brian repeats) on the dog (Brian repeats) again (Brian repeats)." (Big yuks).

"That's the clownie promise, Brian. I can see you're great at following directions, so let's play a game so you can try to win a dollar!" Show the dollar bill to your volunteer and to the audience, then fold it and place it back into the bottom of the chick pan. Pick up the lid and, as I place it on the bottom of the pan, I say, "Let's put the lid on for safe-keeping."

With the lid on, I ask the volunteer to help me by holding the tray. By having the child hold the tray throughout the rest of the routine, you've eliminated the temptation they may have to pick up anything on the tray. You can also have fun when you give him the tray.

Next I instruct Brian, "Put one hand here (direct his left hand to one side of the tray), one hand here (direct his right hand to the other side of the tray), (then I reach behind my magic stand and pull out a fake hand), and one hand here (place the fake hand on the tray in front of the chick pan so the audience sees it)!"

The fake hand is a startling surprise and awesome clown silly business. I act confused, much like I got carried away by the momentum of adding hands to hold the tray. I take the fake hand off the tray and do a Jack Benny-like pose, placing the hand on the side of my face. If you don't know who Jack Benny is, visit YouTube.

Just imagine, all this interaction and funny business with your volunteer, and the trick hasn't even happened yet!

Now it's time to get to the challenge at hand and find out if and how he will try to win a genuine dollar.

"Okay Brian, to try to win a dollar, I will ask you a few questions. To make this game easy, Brian, I'll give you the correct answers to the questions, and the correct answer to all the questions is (pause) PEANUTS! The audience laughs at this. I ask the volunteer to practice saying PEANUTS! nice and loud, so everyone can hear. The volunteer does so, repeating after me, and, giggles.

I put my hand on the volunteer's shoulder, or just on their back. This shows your encouragement and reinforces that they are doing just fine.

"Brian, here comes your first question. "What did you have for breakfast today?"

He will pause, giggle, then say "PEANUTS!" If he gives an honest answer, such as pancakes, or Cheerios, I whisper Peanuts to the volunteer, and he will respond Peanuts, during this effect.

Continue with several more questions. Here are samples:

1. What did you have for lunch (PEANUTS!)... and for dinner? (PEANUTS!) . . . and what's your favorite thing to eat? (PEANUTS!)... and what would you rather eat, ice cream or peanuts? (PEANUTS!)

2. What size shoe do your wear? (as I hold up my big clown shoes for all to see)...(PEANUTS!)

3. What do Mom and Dad give you for an allowance? PEANUTS!)

4. What kind of car do you drive?...What do you say when girls chase you? . . . What did you get on your report card?.. ETC!

Sometimes your volunteer will giggle so much that he can barely say "PEANUTS!" I always echo the answer, "PEANUTS!" after the volunteer has said it. I laugh along with everyone, not at the volunteer, and I tell the volunteer throughout all this that he's doing just great and that he's the star of the show!

Four or five questions, depending on the response, are enough, then I ask the big question. I look straight ahead (an innocent, starry-eyed look) and gesture in a big way with my hands as I ask, "Brian, is there anything else (short pause) in the whooole world (short pause) you would rather have (short pause) other than a dollar bill?"

I continue to look straight ahead, allowing the audience to laugh at the anticipation. The volunteer almost always hesitates before saying, "PEANUTS!" It's that hesitation and my starry-eyed look that gets the yuks here.

When the volunteer says "PEANUTS!" my mouth drops open, and I ask (in disbelief) the audience, "Did he say PEANUTS?!"

(Note: It doesn't matter what final answer the volunteer gives. Peanuts will always appear. If he has been saying "PEANUTS!" all along and doesn't give that answer I can cover by saying, "You said Peanuts! so many times we got Peanuts!" I never tell them they gave the wrong answer). That is why it doesn't matter what the kid says for their final answer.

This reminds me of the time I used a four-year-old as a volunteer for Peanuts! She followed directions until I asked if there was anything she'd rather have than the dollar. There was a long pause, silence and anticipation in the audience. She matter-of-factly replied, "A Trans-Am." Nothing could have been any funnier! Everyone, including me, fell out laughing!

The audience confirms that the volunteer said, "PEANUTS!" and I say, "Let's check!" I remove the chick pan lid, spill all those peanuts onto the tray, and say (cheerfully and confidently), "You got peanuts!" As I say that, I am placing the empty chick pan bottom behind my magic stand.

(Note: Spilling the peanuts on the tray, rather than just lifting off the chick pan lid to reveal the peanuts, is an important move here. If you leave the peanuts in the pan, the audience will assume that the dollar bill is under them. Spilling the peanuts is a super visual climax, adds noise, and shows the chick pan empty, proving the dollar bill has vanished and turned into peanuts).

After audience response has subsided, I say, "Wow! You must have said "PEANUTS!" so many times, you magically turned that dollar bill into peanuts! But Brian, I have a huge prize for you for being such a wondiferous Clownie for a Day!"

I show an over-sized fake dollar bill and announce that because Brian is such a big-time assistant, he gets a tiny dollar bill. The children always correct me, letting me know it's too big.

Don't even think of not giving your "Peanuts!" volunteer a souvenir, over-sized, funny dollar bill. It would be very disappointing to the volunteer to get nothing, and that would make this routine seem mean. The kid earned that dollar! I taught another magician this routine, and he discovered that he only felt comfortable with it if he gives the child the real dollar bill anyway after the trick. However, in my experience, the volunteer is not disappointed at not receiving the genuine dollar because the over-sized one is special, unique, and something only he receives.

I send the volunteer back to his seat as I thank him and ask the audience to give him a big round of applesauce, oops I mean applause! The parents think it's funny when I remind them that the gift tax is already paid on the dollar.

I don't give the peanuts to the volunteer. The funnee-munee seems to be enough, and parents don't like peanut shells ground into the carpet! If I'm doing the routine in an outdoor show, I might hand out the peanuts.

I have had excellent results and a lot of fun with Peanuts! Whenever I ask children what their favorite part of my show is they always mention Peanuts! first. Close seconds are juggling and the live bunny rabbit. I would think the bunny would be the favorite, but what do I know? They're the audience, so they're the judges. The kids laugh with more than the usual laughter during this routine. It is a lot of fun to experience the children and the volunteer laughing so hard they can't stop! I tell them they need to stop being so sad and cheer up! (More yuks.)

(Note: Each child at the party gets a funny mystery dollar later in the party. It also has magic tricks kids can do printed on the back. However, since I give each child at my shows one of my mystery dollars, I looked for something different for this "Peanuts!" volunteer. I give him a phony dollar which is larger and noticeably different from what the others receive. The super humongous dollar bills are impressive.

Also, some people have peanut allergies. Always check with the host before using peanuts in this trick, or select another treat, such as sugar-free wrapped candies. Then you would change the magic word, Peanuts! to the word Candy!

If you're not confident about doing magic tricks, a chick pan requires no skill. It's how you play the routine, your comic timing, and audience interaction that makes this trick an audience favorite.

"With comedy, you have no place to go but more comedy, so you're never off the hook."

— Steve Martin

Chapter 11
Vanilla, The Wondiferous Wonder Bunny

Magically producing a bunny rabbit at the end of a show has traditionally been a magician's trick. However, for clowns, producing a live rabbit offers a dynamic dimension to our shows that can only delight our audiences and help ensure repeat bookings and referrals. Even if you're primarily a clown or a puppeteer, storyteller, ventriloquist, or a juggler, a live bunny will add that extra something special to your shows.

Rabbits best suited for shows are French mini lops, Netherland dwarfs and Dutch bunnies. They tend to stay small, so will fit into magic production boxes easily. Check with magic dealers for suggestions on rabbit effects and production equipment.

Before we get into rabbit comedy, I should remind you that on those hot summer days when you're performing outdoors, you should prep your bunny in the production equipment at the last possible moment before show time and place the production box in a well-shaded area. Better yet, if you perform with a partner or assistant, have them set the illusion up just prior to that portion of your show.

I've been careful when booking shows to let the host know that the show must take place in a shaded area. This is for everyone's comfort—the audience, the bunny, and myself, the clown wearing full wardrobe, makeup and a wig. My preference is to perform indoors.

Story Line for Surprise

I always figured that if I told the audience I could make a rabbit appear, there wouldn't be much of an element of surprise when I made it happen. Instead, I asked the audience if they would like to help me try to make an elephant appear. No adults have fainted yet.

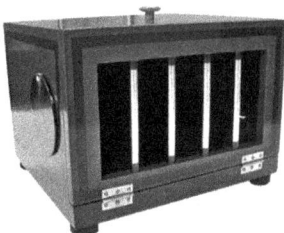

My production box is a table-top Pagoda. I show it empty, and then I check the door on the top by peeking inside. I yell "Yikes!" as if I am surprised by what's in the box and laugh. Then announce, "As sure as elephants love peanuts, there is an elephant in there!" I check the top of the box again, yell "Yikes, the elephant is on roller skates!" "What? You don't believe me?" I open the top door again and produce a small elephant on wheels, a Christmas tree ornament. Yes, there are laughs and groans.

"Well, it is an elephant!" Then I check the front panel again. It still seems to be an empty box. I ask the audience to say the magic words, "Have a banana!" as I check the top of the box.

You can produce spring flowers, or foam magic props, even a wireless umbrella, in addition to producing the bunny later in the routine, all from the same production box.

We try to make the elephant appear again. "I know what we forgot. We forgot to wave the magic wand." The guest of honor is an excellent choice for a volunteer. Nesting wands are a good choice to use here, as are rubber fish or chickens as wands. Make a spectacle out of the magic words. The magnificent moment is about to happen.

Vanilla the Wondiferous Wonder Bunny appears, but I haven't looked yet, because I'm standing to the side of the Pagoda. I think I've produced an elephant, and the kids are excited, jumping, laughing, yelling "It's a rabbit!"

Then I glance, do a double-take, and I am just as surprised as the audience because my intention was to make an elephant appear.

"It's not an elephant, but it's the next best thing—my friend Vanilla the Wondiferous Wonder Bunny!"

There is no disappointment that an elephant didn't appear, although the adults are relieved.

Audience Control

When Vanilla magically appears, there is excitement, oohs and ahhs, and children will rush to pet her. I head them off at the pass, letting them know that everyone will have a chance to pet Vanilla.

While the children are settling down, I stroke Vanilla's back and share a few fascinating facts about Vanilla.

- Vanilla the Wondiferous Wonder Bunny is very lucky. Do you know why? No? She has four rabbit's feet!

- Vanilla is a Dutch bunny. She doesn't speak much English!

- I know Vanilla looks a little pale. She recently had an hoperation!

- Vanilla the Wondiferous Wonder Bunny is going to beauty school. She's becoming a hare dresser!

- Do you know what you get when you cross Vanilla the Wondiferous Wonder Bunny and an insect? Bugs Bunny.

- I've been trying to find out how Vanilla the Wondiferous Wonder Bunny magically appears. She might have hopped a bus, or she might be an ingrown hare!

- Do you know how I met Vanilla? One day I opened my refrigerator and Vanilla was just sitting there. That's right, Vanilla was in my fridge, just sitting there. I asked her, "What are you doing in my refrigerator?" Vanilla replied, "This is a Westinghouse isn't it?" Puzzled, I said, "Yes, it is." Vanilla smiled and said, "Well, I'm just westing!"

Instructions for Petting the Rabbit

"Before you pet Vanilla, there are special rules. Do you know what they are? No?"

"Well you can't poke her in the eye, or pull her ears, or put your fingers in her face. Do you know why?" Sometimes the children will say that poking would hurt Vanilla. "Well that's true, but the main reason you shouldn't poke Vanilla, is that it will ruin her whoooole day."

Children pet the bunny one at a time. Children may want to hold Vanilla, which I don't accommodate. Vanilla could scratch the child or hop away.

Children sometimes ask if they can keep Vanilla. I explain that we are partners and she is under contract to magically appear at our shows and that she has other families to visit.

Exit Line

After allowing children to pet Vanilla one at a time, I explain that she needs to retire to her dressing room to take a union break and munch on carrot cake. (Jest kidding.)

Magically producing a live bunny during my show for many years increased my opportunities for more business and referrals. A live bunny magically appearing is a keen sales feature, guaranteed to leave the audience in laughter and awe.

The letters I've received from children over the years prove that Vanilla the Wondiferous Wonder Bunny left families with fond memories.

*"If you see with innocent eyes,
everything is divine."*

—Federico Fellini

Chapter 12
Picnics with Pizazz

Whether you're performing at a large corporate picnic or for a city recreation department, you will need to program your time and show so you don't use all your energy in the first hour.

How long is long enough? Most corporate picnics I performed at were three-hour engagements. That seemed to be long enough to do all the activities I planned, yet isn't so long I would be thoroughly exhausted. And we want to appear as though we are full of energy.

If a group has fewer than 300 guests attending, I book the engagement for a two-hour minimum. You need to know how long you can entertain under the hot sun. Don't book yourself for a four- or five-hour appearance outdoors if you don't think you can survive it in fine style. Book the five-hour engagement, but split the hours with another performer so you are both fresh and energized. I program my corporate picnic activities and have had success, but keep in mind you will want to personalize your own picnic program.

Meet and Greet

Most picnic chairpersons want a clown to meet and greet guests as they arrive. This helps break the ice and let people know they are in for a fun day. Often there is one person in a family attending who knows many of the other people at the picnic. The spouse and children may not know any-one else outside their own family. Welcoming the guests, making them feel comfortable, and directing them to the picnic area makes a positive difference.

For a three-hour picnic, I meet and greet for about thirty minutes. I welcome everyone and let them know I will be there for a while and what time I will do my show. This helps them plan their day in the park.

Come and Get It

After the meet and greet, the caterers are ready to serve lunch. I take advantage of having a truly captive audience with lots of folks standing in line. I perform walk-arounds with the aid of some over-sized props and all the physical and verbal comedy I can come up with.

One of the favorite crowd pleasers, while people are waiting in line, is trying to deliver an over-sized foam sandwich to someone who must have ordered it. There is a lot of funny business and by-play which makes this a visual walk-around and it gets big yuks. Best of all, it keeps the guests entertained if they're waiting in line.

At a picnic, you will find that not everyone is eating at the same time. You could visit tables where people have just finished their meal first. Bring a puppet, close-up magic, or havefunny business prepared in case you meet up with a shy group.

One of my favorite close-up magic tricks is the Sponge Bunny routine, requiring two seconds of setup that you can do in your pocket. Check out the full routine in Chapter 9.

Let the guests know when and where your show will begin.

It's Show Time

After lunch is a good time to do a show. The guests don't want to run a relay race, so sitting down and relaxing is a good choice. Ask the picnic chairperson to announce that your show will begin in five minutes, and where it will be. This will help to gather the crowd.

I suppose you could get away without doing a show, but it establishes you as a performer, and people enjoy seeing a prepared show rather than only walk-arounds for several hours. I have also noticed that many people will ask you for a business card after the show. Consider this an audition for your next birthday party, corporate picnic, Christmas party, or family reunion.

Your show should comprise your skills and talents. Are you a storyteller? Puppeteer? Magician? Juggler? Unicyclist? A combination of several of these categories? I perform a thirty-minute show which begins with a juggling warm-up done to circus music. This warm-up gets the audience in the mood for the show and fires me up. The main part of my show comprises comedy magic with the aid of audience volunteers.

After the show, I enjoy clowning with the parents and kids who hang around while I'm packing the show.

The Closer

After the show, I have about thirty to forty minutes to wind things down at the picnic. I perform sight gags. A sight gag is something that your audience can see is funny from a distance as you walk around. They don't have to be right there in your space to get the joke.

An example of a solid walk-around is using an invisible dog leash. However, I place a large foam carved hot dog on a bun inside the harness. Now I have Frank the Dawg. People from afar can enjoy this sight-gag, and people close-by get the one-liners: I explain that Frank relished the idea of being in show business, but he couldn't cut the mustard. I'd let Frank pull me, then yell, "I have to ketchup!" You could even add a dog name tag and a dog license on your foam hot dog. The jingling of the two tags make it sound like a real dog approaching. (See Chapter 4 for The Big Wheel and Clown at Wurk).

During the last hour of the picnic or at closing time, you could produce balloon sculptures, work with a puppet, or perform close-up magic.

The reason you wouldn't want to do balloons before the last hour is because you can get very tied down to the activity. It is very difficult to move around and create a wonderful high-energy atmosphere when you have thirty or more kids all wanting a balloon.

The line will seem to be eternal. If you produce balloons too early in the picnic, many will burst, and you will have a constant stream of children wanting another one. It will cut into your walk-around time during the lunch line. Once someone sees you make a balloon sculpture, they see no reason you can't continue to make twenty more, and right now.

Handy Tips

Take short breaks every hour in the hot summer months. It's best not to take your break among clients or to eat with them. I bring bottled water and take my short break in my vehicle, parked away from the picnic activity. It is very important to drink plenty of water to keep from getting dehydrated. There is nothing funny about a dehydrated clown passing out. I also take this opportunity to leave props I've been using and pick up new ones.

Ask the picnic chairperson if they want you to do anything extra such as host a watermelon eating contest, announce winners of door prizes or gather groups of people for special activities.

Keep in mind you are special entertainment for the day. If the picnic chairperson wants balloons, face painting, games, and shows going on all at once, advise them to engage more than one or two clowns or performers for the day.

Have fun. You're a star!

"In the end, everything is a gag."

— Charlie Chaplin

Chapter 13
Clowns Taste Funny

When I lived in Maryland, I entertained at a local pizza parlor for two hours on Sundays. The owner wanted to cultivate a family night, and since his Sunday nights were slow, he used me in that time slot. He did his part with consistent local advertising of the times and dates of my appearances. Sunday evenings soon turned into a solid family night. Many patrons would be sure to bring their children and friends. That engagement lasted five years.

This gig is great for the clown or any entertainer establishing a clientele, experience, and exposure, and wants to fine tune skills and confidence with the public.

At places like pizza and ice cream parlors, you'll be relying on walk-around, meet-and-greet entertaining; you'll be working table-to-table with several groups of people, not doing a full-blown, structured show. You'll gain the chance to get yourself better known, which will strengthen your bookings, and you'll have a steady gig.

The Pitch

The first step is finding a restaurant that suits you and convincing the owner or manager that your appearances will translate to more profit. Be prepared to smile and make your case.

I also used to clown at an ice cream parlor. One of the first things I said to the owner was, "Kids and clowns and ice cream are a perfect match." He liked that.

Let the restaurant owner or manager know that your presence will help create a wholesome image, entice more parents to bring their kids, and give customers even happier memories. You can, like I did, help build a strong family night on what may have been a slow time. If the reply is, "We're busy, packed all the time," you will respond by reminding the owner or manager that people are often at their grouchiest when they're hungry and waiting. Your entertainment can help take their minds off their hunger and wait time, resulting in happier customers sure to return.

In a nutshell, you're offering a promotion gimmick that, if advertised, will bring more families to their restaurant. You serve as a customer relations rep that will keep customers happier and help bring them back.

So how do you get noticed? Do your homework first. Visit restaurants as a regular customer. Observe the atmosphere, the clientele, and general operation. Collect your data and thoughts. Consider how you would benefit this restaurant. Now you're ready to contact the owner or manager.

I found it best not to phone ahead and ask for an interview. Owners and managers won't make time for you, and it's easier to brush you off on the phone. The most effective way to make initial contact is through a referral.

If that's not possible, wear business casual attire, and go to the restaurant between 2 and 3 p.m. If you approach the owner or manager during lunch or dinner hours, you'll turn them off, so plan your visit.

Introduce yourself to the owner or manager saying something like, "May I talk to you for a moment about a promotional idea for your restaurant?"

Keep this initial contact professional and brief. Present your edit portfolio including letters of recommendation and large photographs, in color, of your clown character. Leave the owner or manager with samples of your balloon modeling or show a short magic trick, have your puppet say hello, etc. Leave your photograph with your phone number. The owner or manager may have to consult with a partner, owner, or manager before deciding, so any visual aids can only help your pitch.

Offer to audition for about a half an hour during his business hours, at the time they would consider booking you for. This gives the owner or manager the opportunity to observe you in character. It also shows your positive, team-player attitude. Your audition is just that, no fee, and no obligation to the owner or manager.

The Audition: You're On, Kid!

Enter in character. There are six tables with patrons out of twenty tables. What do I do first? Wave and say, "Hi," to all. Attend to the guests at tables with children first. As you are entertaining the children, parents may ask, "Wow! What's the occasion?"

You'll answer in clown character style, "This is my audition here at Pizza Haven (as you're twisting a balloon for the children or doing other funny-business), and if you like what I do and think it's a good idea to have me here regularly, I would appreciate your telling the owner or manager on your way out."

You have by this time clowned your little heart out, told funny stories and cracked one-liners throughout your balloon modeling, performed at least one small magical miracle, and given your attention and personal warmth, at least for a moment, to every person in that restaurant.

Some of my favorite interactions with kids went like this: "What's your name? Andrew? That was my name when I was a little boy." Laughs from the parents, confused kid faces, and comments like, "You're a girl," prompted me to reply, "Naw, I'm an elephant in disguise."

"How old are you? Eight? What grade are you in? Third? Three years old and in the eighth grade?! You must be smart!" Kids will waste no time in telling you you're mixed up and correct you.

If the child is younger than five I might shake their hand, and wiggle their arm, while asking them, "Are you nervous? There's Jell-O in that arm." Young kids giggle.

As you leave each table, mention something like, "I sure hope you had good food and fun here at Pizza Haven today, and we hope you'll come again." Remember, your job is to promote the restaurant. Management likes to hear their name reinforced. Plus, as you say the restaurant's name, customers are connecting you with the restaurant.

Remember to connect with the servers, the cook, and the owner or manager, too. Give them a few moments, too. Joke, send a balloon sculpture home for their kids, etc. You want them on your side.

You Landed the Gig

Your audition was a smashing success, and you're hired. You have an opportunity and responsibility to assist this business in building family clientele, during the hours you're booked.

The owner or manager's advertising commitment and how they intend to use you will help you set a fee. Decide on the hours you will spend on the floor entertaining. My Sunday night Pizza Parlor gig ran from 5 to 7 p.m. and in the summer, 6 to 8 p.m.

Consider a Trial Period

In both restaurants I worked for, it was clear the owner or manager wanted to hire me. I considered my audition a show of my goodwill. However, if an owner or manager wants to book you for a trial period, be sure it's long enough. Two weeks, for example, isn't enough. No one will see any real changes. Eight to ten weeks is a more realistic time frame.

Advertising

One of the most important ingredients for your mutual success is advertising. Most owners and managers will already plan on this. If they aren't, let them know you'll both lose. Word of mouth advertising is always one of the best forms of advertising, but in this situation, it isn't enough.

The owner or manager will presumably run ads in the local paper. You can facilitate this by supplying the owner or manager with a black-and-white photo (head shots are best) or a black and white line drawing of your clown character. Be sure to clip copies of these ads from the newspaper, because they will be useful tools to help gain future bookings. Promo in the store is also useful. In the restaurants where I entertained, they displayed a large photograph of my clown character along with a sign that showed dates and times of my appearances. It generated interest in the restaurant, more business, and more client referrals for me.

As people left the restaurant, they could pick up my flier and my business card. Both pieces were available at the checkout desk where they paid their check.

I also had a coloring page made of my clown character. The coloring sheet included my phone number and a blurb about my appearances at the restaurant. This marketing collateral reached many people. It was a win-win for both the restaurant and my business.

Your Fee

It is difficult to tell you what your fee should be since every restaurant owner or manager has a different budget for entertainment and advertising. There are a few guidelines that will help you figure out what you should charge.

Consistent employment in a restaurant offers you a great deal of exposure in your community. Any print, social media or radio advertising paid for by the owner can do nothing but good for your entertainment business. Ask yourself what it's worth.

Consider making these engagements affordable enough to the owner so they can have you perform. A price break is in order, so consider your expenses in time, energy, wear and tear on props and balloon costs.

Sometimes performers will entertain at a low fee to the restaurant and make it known tips are welcome. Some will wear a badge suggesting a tip. Others will leave a box or colorful container at the cash register that says "For the Clown." Some restaurants will offer food as part of your compensation.

I prefer to keep the pressure off the guests, so they can enjoy the interaction rather than feel pressure to offer a tip. I worked out a salary arrangement with both restaurants I clowned for. Not performing for tips sends a message to customers that I am present thanks to the hospitality of the restaurant.

My salary at those restaurants wouldn't win any awards in Fortune 500, but the combined results of consistent income, constant public exposure with advertising and referrals made this arrangement well worth the effort.

"Comedy is very controlling. You are making people laugh."

— Gilda Radner

Chapter 14
Would You Like a Side of Clown with that Pizza?

25 Hot Tips for Performing in Restaurants

1. Approach people in a friendly manner. If you are a physical performer, you will want to reel it in for this gig. Yes, on animation. No, on circus-style antics.

2. Visit people waiting for their orders first and those who are waiting to visit with the clown. Don't try to entertain people when they're receiving their meal.

3. Don't interfere with a server who is taking an order or in the midst of delivering orders to the table.

4. Don't blow or pump a balloon over a customer's table. It can burst and end up in their food. I use a pump and inflate balloons away from the table or toward the floor if I'm cramped for space.

5. If a child is scared, move out of their space. If you stand back from the child and wave from a safe distance, you will often ease their fears. Another tactic is to ignore the child, but allow them to see you're entertaining other kids who aren't scared and are having a great time. You can send a balloon animal or coloring sheet via the waitress to the scared child—a peace offering, so to speak, showing you care.

6. Don't give a balloon to a child under three years old without the parents' consent (it's a choking hazard).

7. People will want to chat and ask questions. They expect you to answer as a real person, not the clown. Remember that you're in clown persona. Keep your responses short, clever, and funny and move on to the people waiting.

8. Don't be abrupt in your attempts to get to everyone. This is one-to-one audience close contact performing. Your personal warmth is important for your success.

9. People love to laugh. Treat each person as someone special.

10. Remember people's names. I cultivated that skill during my restaurant days. Customers liked being remembered by name on return visits.

11. Focus on the table you're working with, and use your peripheral vision for staying aware of other tables' reactions at the same time. For example, I performed a magic trick and began by engaging a table of people, then realized people from nearby tables were interested.

12. Involve observers from other tables if they show interest. After I departed, I observed that those tables of people were now speaking with each other even though they had been strangers before they enjoyed the balloon comedy and magic together. Those moments were rewarding.

13. Don't be demanding on your restaurant audience. They are there to dine and enjoy their families and friends. You are a great attraction, but people may not want to stop their conversations and give full attention to a routine. Don't take it as a personal rejection. Smile, say something friendly or funny (not sarcastic), and move on to the next table.

14. Be careful how you present magic in the family restaurant setting. Sucker tricks, where people may get embarrassed at the end, don't make for terrific customer relations. If anyone has to be the brunt of a joke, it should

be you. Keep it light, simple and brief, engaging your audience through comedic interaction and participation.

15. On occasion, I got a heckler—a wise guy who was just showing off for friends with comments. "Hey clown, I wonder what you look like under all that." I stayed in character and responded using humor. I responded, "Have I got a balloon for you!" and created his balloon last (jest desserts). When I got to the heckler, I made his balloon but showed it to everyone else at the table first. (Big yuks). The balloon I made was an orangutan! One time I got a large tip from the heckler as he commented, "You're all right!"

16. Sometimes guests wanted me exclusively at their table. Apply your best people skills to let them know you've enjoyed visiting with them, but now you have more folks to meet and greet. Most people take the hint.

17. Give most of your attention to restaurant patrons but, as in the audition, don't leave out restaurant personnel. Understand their needs, joke with them, be polite. If they're in your corner, they are your allies; if they don't, everyone feels the strain.

18. Along with the experience and exposure restaurant entertaining offers you, it creates more booking opportunities.

19. I don't want to sound like your mother, but since you're working in proximity to people, take extra care with your wardrobe and keep your fingernails clean and filed.

20. Don't handle personal, outside booking business on the restaurant's time. If a patron asks you, and they will, "How much do you charge for birthday parties?" Explain that they can call you and you'll check your availability. Smile and hand them a business card. Your clown persona should not break character to conduct business while you are performing. I have had no one push the issue, and I received many calls for private bookings through restaurant contacts.

21. **A Low-Hassle Audition:** When I got a call from a prospective client who wanted to audition me before hiring my act for a party, special event or picnic, I invited them to come to the restaurant where I play. This confirmed that a business valued my skills enough to use me. Often I booked the job just by giving that information. If they still wanted to preview me, this was a low-hassle opportunity for them to preview my clown character, performance, and people skills.

22. **When It's Not Your Restaurant:** What do you do when you're asked to perform in a restaurant for a private party and it's not the restaurant where you regularly perform? If you're working with another restaurant and are a strong part of their local advertising, you

should honor that commitment. Make sure the owner or manager won't mind if you do a show for a private party in a competitor's establishment. Don't make a big issue out of it, just keep it up front.

23. It's a good idea to ask your client to get prior approval from the proposed restaurant's management. It's a matter of courtesy and, who knows, they may have their own entertainer. One food chain with national characters will not allow outside performers to just come in and entertain, even if the patron so desires.

24. Prior clearance can save everyone heartburn—you, your client and the restaurant. Embarrassment on arrival and in extreme cases of being turned away at the front door can be avoided. Besides, when you get the green light ahead of time, arrive to perform, thank the owne or manager for allowing you to entertain and then ask him if they can catch your show. The owner or manager may keep you in mind and refer his contacts when they're looking for entertainment.

25. The Two-In-One: Sometimes I received calls to do a birthday party. but the client did not have my fee. I offered two solutions.

- *Option 1:* There was a party room in the pizza parlor where I performed. I suggested they hold the party during my performance hours. I clarified that I can treat the birthday child special and make balloon animals at no extra cost, but I will give equal attention to other patrons in the restaurant.

- *Option 2:* The client booked the party in the pizza parlor an hour before my scheduled time. I gave the party my undivided attention and did my usual comedy magic birthday party show with audience participation, goody bags, the works. I charged half of my regular fee. The client got my full show for a discounted fee, the restaurant owner or manger loved that I booked more business, plus I got an extra booking by arriving earlier. This meant applying makeup once for two bookings with no travel time in between. These special arrangements built great client relationships for both the restaurant and myself. Be sure to get the owner or manager's approval before you offer deals to clients.

"The role of a clown and a physician are the same. It's to elevate the possible and to relieve suffering."

—Patch Adams

Chapter 15
Anatomy of a Hospital Clown

One-to-one clowning is a delicate and sensitive art. We all understand that the desire to cheer up sick people is not enough. It takes your thoughtfulness and careful planning to build successful relationships with staff and patients. In this chapter, I'll share approaches and ideas I've learned from my years of experience as a professional clown and from interviews with several hospital public relations directors.

Hospital clowning isn't just about visiting the children. In my experience, there is not much difference in clowning for kids or adults in a hospital setting. Almost everyone needs comic relief and a little fun while in the hospital.

First Stop: Hospital Public Relations Director

Always clear your visit with hospital public relations directors before you visit patients if you're not known there yet. If you aren't greeted with shouts of come on down, don't be disappointed. The first responsibility of the hospital staff is to the well-being of patients. One P.R. director told me, "We have to make sure you're not a kook or trying to sell patients a product or way of life."

One way to handle the situation is to arrange a time to meet with the P.R. director as yourself, in street clothes. Bring your clown photos. You'll be able to show your sincerity, establish trust, and dispel any concerns.

This is a good time to mention that one P.R. director said she sometimes receives calls from people who want to clown with difficult cases. She wastes no time in saying "No," and adds that you need special training or close teamwork with trained people to get into this field. She commented that the desire to charge in and remedy the lives of troubled people is not the way to begin.

P.R. directors and the hospital staff have one focus: Their patients' safety and well-being.

Check In with the head nurse

After you get clearance, check in with the staff of every floor and wing of the hospital before visiting any patients. The first question to ask the head nurse is, "Who should I visit first?"

Someone might be in isolation or too ill to receive a visit from a clown. You need to know which rooms to avoid, or maybe wave to a patient through an isolation window. The nurses know their patients' ever-changing status and will want to direct you to certain people they feel will enjoy your visit.

A Lesson in Cooperation

I'll never forget, in my hospital rounds as Dokter Funnybone, when the Doctors and nurses explained a difficult patient's case. I'll call him Dan. He was about 45, a prominent attorney, and he had suffered a near-fatal heart attack.

He was so angry about his heart attack he wouldn't speak to hospital staff. They asked if I would try to visit him. I agreed since the hospital staff felt confident in my abilities. I entered Dan's room, smiled and announced, "Hello, I'm Dokter Funnybone, new on your case. How are you feeling today?"

Yes, I know I took a big chance with this entrance, but this patient was different. Dan just looked at me with a confused, are-you-kidding-expression. Dan's eyes, however, showed a spark of interest, even though he remained silent.

Visiting with Dan became three of the longest minutes of my life until I pulled out my balloon pump. His facial expression changed from stubborn and angry with one of inquisitiveness. As I held the balloon pump up for inspection, I stated, "Oh this? It's intravenous clown, and your diet needs this vitamin," as I smiled and looked into his eyes. Dan smiled back. I squeezed his hand and reminded him that the doctors and nurses cared and were trying to help him. He nodded, and I left.

The staff had watched us through an observation window. They said it was the best response Dan had shown since he was admitted. Only then, I learned that Dan had ordered everyone out of his room, until I visited him.

Your Entrance: Read the Room

Dan is a splendid example of working with staff and of doing the best you can to be sensitive to the situations as they happen. Once you get to a patient's door, there aren't any set formulas, but there are clear signals to watch for.

When drapes are closed around the bed area, it's a clear sign the patient may be asleep and needs privacy. Respect the closed space; don't intrude. If a doctor comes in to check on a patient while you're visiting, leave. Their conversation is private and should be free of distractions. You can visit other patients and then go back to revisit those you had to leave.

Other signals aren't so clear, and your intuitive awareness of how your clown visit is affecting someone is critical. Start out low-key. Don't make a noisy entrance. Even though it was perfect for a party or circus entrance, this arena requires sensitivity. Peek in the doorway, or stick your big foot or a puppet to get the patient's attention. Use your peripheral vision to check for IV's and available playing space. Gauge the patient's physical condition and their reaction to you. Let them invite you in. Dan's case was an exception.

Play your full clown character only if you see and feel the opportunity. Some people are up for your gags and comic relief but don't overstay your welcome or wear them out.

Others may be like the lady flat on her back, pale and still. I asked her how she felt and she answered, "Very weak." I held her hand for a while and said, "You rest. I hope you feel better real soon. Goodbye." She nodded but her eyes told me she appreciated the visit. If I had insisted on cheering her up, doing one-liners and gags, it may have caused a drain on her already low energy. We both knew we cared.

Be prepared for the possibility of rejection. Contrary to popular belief, all the world does not love a clown. If someone shows hostility or just isn't up to your visit, leave.

Be Present in the Face of Sadness

As I entered one room, a frail and elderly man was sitting in a wheelchair. He was in his 70s. Both legs were in casts.

When I tried to talk to him, I realized we would have communication difficulties. He had also suffered a stroke.

His speech was slurred, but he kept trying to say something, even through his tears. I was patient and stayed with him. It took six attempts before I understood what he was trying to tell me. That day was his fiftieth wedding anniversary and he could not go home to be with his wife. He sobbed uncontrollably.

I told him I was so sorry that he couldn't be with his wife. I wondered if my presence was upsetting him. I asked him if would like me to go. He grasped my hand right away, held it tight and sobbed as he pleaded, "No." This broken-hearted elderly man just wanted me to keep him company. I thought I had come to the hospital to bring a little cheer, but I was wrong. He needed someone to sit with him, so I made a quick decision, to be the friend he needed. I stayed for a long time, stroking his hand.

I learned from this patient that if I wanted to be a hospital clown, I had to give people the right to cry and laugh with me and that both are okay. This man felt safe with me, so he revealed his true feelings. Comfort was what he needed most.

I was honored to be walking in the shoes of a clown.

Assisting a Patient

Don't! If a patient asks for a glass of water, you don't know if that drink could postpone surgery another twenty-four hours. If you help a patient turn over in bed, you don't know their physical condition; they could pull a muscle, or worse. Even though helping when you're asked may seem harmless and the caring thing to do, tell the patient you'll call for one of the staff to give a hand.

Silent Clowns

If you're a silent clown, don't be rigid about keeping silent. We need to be more sensitive to patients than to the rigors of an art form in the hospital situation. There may be a time when you sense that a person needs to talk, hear a voice, or isn't up to the effort of interpreting your movements. For all of us, I think we need to remember that a one-to-one visit is more of an act of love than a performance. Clowning is the means, not the end.

Doctors and the Medical Staff

Remember to acknowledge and entertain these hard-working professionals, but don't hold them up with your act. Let them get back to their work.

Do Not Dispense Medical Advice

Do not inquire about specifics of anyone's condition. Do not even ask why they are in the hospital. And never, ever, ever offer medical advice, or speak of any of personal stories about health, pain, medications, or anything you may feel can help the patient. You would break clown character to discuss health issues.

More importantly, dispensing advice or telling health stories would be a blatant misuse of your privilege to visit patients as a clown. This could cause unnecessary anxiety for the patient, not to mention possible legal implications.

Your job description in the hospital setting is to lift the spirits of the patients if you can. Leave medical stories out of the mix and let the health care professionals do their job.

Holidays

When you are thinking of times to do hospital visiting, consider going at times that aren't holidays. One volunteer director told me entertainers want to visit on holidays but forget about patients the rest of the year. Once I knew this, I decided to visit the hospital more frequently during the year.

Keep in mind that hospital funny-business is wonderful used at the right time and with the right patient. You will find light moments and some difficult ones. Trust yourself.

Sometimes being that special visitor who cared enough to be with them is enough. Maybe the patient just needs to talk and you need to listen, not entertain. Use your judgment and be sensitive to their moods.

Hospital clowning is special, and it may not be for everyone. I do it because I know the genuine receiver is me.

Patient Funny Business

Add Dr. or "Dokter" to your clown name/badge. Be mindful that Doctors have earned the right to call themselves "doctor" which is why I use "Dokter." That also lets the professionals know you respect their hard-earned titles. Wear a doctor's lab coat over your clown wardrobe.

Make a silly light deflector with a headband and a pot pie tin. Carry a small bag with doctor-like gadgets. Toy medical kits can be fun too.

Place your stethoscope everywhere but the right place. Place it on your wristwatch and say, "Ah, we're still ticking!"

Show someone your gall stones. Use a pet rock. On the flip side paint, "Made in France."

Holding a tongue depressor, ask the patient to open wide and say "AHH." As they do, you look into the mouth of somebody nearby (a nurse, another clown, a visitor). Then look at the patient giving thumbs up, saying, "You're Okay!"

Prescribe funny prescriptions and add P.R.N. (that's doctor speak for "as needed").

"I remain just one thing, and one thing only, and that is a clown. It places me on a far higher plane than any politician."

— Charlie Chaplin

Chapter 16
Clown Control at the White House

Clownies who wake up by 4 a.m. don't feel hilarious, but this day was special. It was Easter at the White House, 1986. Joining me were some of Washington, D.C.'s finest and funniest—Becky "Rainbow" Santora and Barry "Bonzo" DeChant, adding color and excitement to the annual Easter egg roll on the South Lawn of the White House. Even though we were up before the sun, some strong coffee and the excitement helped us get into character.

By 6 a.m. we had checked into the White House grounds and had passed through the airport-like detectors. Yes, the guards got a chuckle digging through all of our clown prop bags.

The White House seemed more beautiful than I had remembered it from my years living in Washington, D.C. During 1982, I was invited to perform when Nancy Reagan celebrated her book, *To Love A Child,* about the Foster Grandparents program. More than six hundred foster grandparents and children were bused in from all over the area to enjoy lunch and entertainment. The lawn was green and lush, and at that early hour with no one there, it was perfect for picture taking.

Back to Easter 1986. Our mission included leading a parade for the White House staff, complete with Willard Scott, antique cars, and the official Easter Bunny, before the gates opened to the public. By 9 a.m. the grounds were open and our real mission began.

We were to welcome and greet people, direct them to the egg hunt and roll, and distribute helium balloons. Handing out those helium balloons for two hours became a quick survival lesson in crowd control. We were overwhelmed at first by adults pushing and shoving, with a me-first attitude, just to get a helium balloon.

As Rainbow explained, "Parents were trampling small children to get a balloon for their child. Parents pulled the ribbons from my hands, my hands bled, and I had to tell them to stop or I would have to let the balloons loose. I reminded them about the spirit of Easter. It was just a free helium balloon. But they would do anything to get one. Amazing. I did not like having to break character for self-protection."

I had visions of the next day's *Washington Post* headlines reading: "Freebie Attack, Clownies Mauled at White House."

What can we do if we're caught in a crowd-crunching situation like this one?

I hope the solutions we improvised will be of service to you.

First, define a boundary. This will bring order to the chaos. In the White House situation, I found a roped off area and stood next to it. A Secret Service man was standing close by, which also helped. I let the balloons cascade over the roped area, and it was easier for me to pull some to hand out, without having people taking them from the balloon bouquet I was holding.

Second, the more insistent and pushy the adults became, the more I gave priority to small children. I smiled and said something like, "We have little people here who have been waiting patiently, and this is their day." The children got balloons first, then the adults.

Third, get beyond the push and adrenalin of the crowd and remember to give a personal greeting no matter how brief. When I handed each child a balloon, I made sure they knew I saw them by looking in their eyes and greeting them, even if it was just to say have a fun day or Happy Easter.

Fourth, do your best to take control and not let the crowd control you. For example, I ran out of balloons several times and had to go back to get more. At one point, I realized I had run out just as it was the turn of a young boy who had been waiting. I asked Jason to wait for me and said I would be right back with a balloon for him. I think he wondered if I would return because there was so much activity and so many people on the South Lawn of the White House. Moving through that intense crowd of people who wanted all the balloons was no easy task, so I held the balloons high above my head and I charged forward through the crowd and didn't stop until I got to my destination. Jason got his balloon, and he seemed surprised that I returned.

After the balloons were distributed, we were free to roam the grounds and play with the guests. Now that was fun. People were standing in long lines to wait for the Easter egg hunt and the egg roll, and there was something exciting happening on the stage (magician Doug Henning performed), so there were lots of families to enjoy and entertain. We concentrated on meet-and-greet clowning and lots of funny-business. We had a blast taking pictures with families and signing autographs on their souvenir programs.

By 2:30 p.m. activities were winding down, and so were we. We had one more detail to take care of: helping hand out goody bags to all the guests as they left. Control was established. The bags were available at the South Gate where everyone left, and a sign set the rules: "Goody Bags / One per child, 8 years old and under."

As we left the White House, the grounds appeared almost as empty as they were when we arrived at 6 a.m. A sense of relief washed over me, mixed with melancholy because our mission was over. I was honored to be there with my clown colleagues and take part in a celebration at the White House.

"I thought I would dress in baggy pants, big shoes, a cane and a derby hat, everything a contradiction: the pants baggy, the coat tight, the hat small and the shoes large."

—Charlie Chaplin

Chapter 17
The Sole of a Clown

About the only information I've ever seen written about large comedy clown shoes is that we should have them. Comfort and appearance are important, and since we're on our feet performing, I think the subject deserves more attention.

For many of us, purchasing oversized leather clown shoes shows an emotional and financial commitment to clowning. It is equivalent to vowing, "I will work at being a good clown for a long time."

There are definite advantages to large clown shoes:

1. They are funny looking and attention-getting.
2. They inspire us to develop a unique and silly walk which helps define our characters.
3. They help project a crisp and professional appearance.
4. They are impressive to our clients and sponsors.
5. The public likes and may even expect to see them.

Some of you may feel the way Peter Hines from Rochester, Michigan, felt about clown shoes. "When I clowned four years ago," Peter told me, "I felt that the only true clowns had professional clown shoes. The rest of us were just part-time amateurs.

"As I got more involved with clowning, I wanted those shoes but felt they were an extravagance. One summer I used part of my clown show earnings to purchase those shoes. I was so excited the day they arrived."

Peter's clown characters are Silly, a party clown, and Sorry, a tramp character. He continued his clown shoe story to say "Big shoes gave me that extra confidence, but once I gained the confidence, I discovered I was funny wearing any shoe. I realized I don't have to own clown shoes to be a real clown."

Peter's story reminds me of the opportunity I had several years ago to spend time with the great Danny Chapman and see his clown performance with the circus at the Smithsonian. Danny was funny and gentle in his approach and made everyone feel they were the most important person in his audience. He was a world-class clown. He wore simple blue sneakers.

Not everyone's clown character will require big clown shoes, and other considerations may come into play. For example, you may not want the hassle of changing shoes every time you drive a car if you do several scheduled appearances the same day. You may be in a variety show or a circus which requires several wardrobe changes. Big shoes might get in the way.

Big clown shoes can be dangerous jumping on a mini trampoline or even leaping from stage to do a chase. With large shoes, every step must be deliberate, which can be funny. If I am performing a physical comedy gag with a partner, I am more likely to trip over my feet just because of the sheer volume of the shoe. If the gag requires me to do the old kick-in-the-pants-routine, I have a lot of weight and volume to lift if I wear big shoes, so I wear colorful Converse sneakers instead.

Speaking of sneakers, if you don't own clown shoes yet because of the cost involved or if you want to save wear and tear on our shoes as a rainy-day alternative, try some of the following ideas.

Keep your eyes peeled for the big discount stores for colorful high-top sneakers. I've been lucky enough to find red and purple gems for under $10 a pair. At those prices, buy two pairs and save one for later.

Some clowns have good luck with a size 17 sneaker. Stuff the toes with newspaper or foam and insert a sneaker which fits our foot inside the 17. You can dye them if you purchase natural-colored sneakers.

Try a pair of Converse brand multi-colored, high-top sneakers. One side is green, the other purple, there is an orange stripe on the back and a red tongue. This *Converse-sation* is colorful. He who groans last didn't get the pun.

If you're classic white-face, or Pierrot, and want a more petite look, ballet slippers are a good choice for ladies. They come in white, pink, or black. You'll replace them every six months. In winter and other bad weather, wear sneakers to the gig, then change shoes on arrival to save wear and tear.

For both men and women, another superb choice for a classic look is flat leather jazz shoes found at dancewear stores or online. Comfort and flexibility are their strong points. If you're a traditional Auguste buffoon, however, this look won't work for your character. Sometimes a thrift store will have shoes. For example, Jan Bergesen found a pair with a leather sole which extended to cover a squared-off toe. Jan dyed the shoes red, added yellow laces, and zowie, for less than eight dollars she has funny shoes. She said the dye cost more than the shoes. But if you buy old shoes, dye, and laces, give it your best shot, and it doesn't work the first time around, your investment loss will be minimal.

All the shoes I wear for performance are delegated solely (sorry for the pun) for clowning only. I like having big clown shoes and funny-looking sneakers so I can choose for the demands of the show. Good shoe stores sell cushioned and molded shoe pads which will add comfort to any shoe.

Now, if you decide that big clown shoes are what you want and they suit your character, go for it and take care of them. When your brand-new, all-leather, oversized shoes arrive, take them to your local shoe repair shop to have a leather patch applied to the sole at the ball of the shoe. This portion of the sole takes an extra beating.

Also, every year before and after my busy company picnic season, I take my clown shoes to the local shoe repairman to have them refurbished. He checks and repairs the seams, the soles and any wear on the inside. Caring for these shoes by polishing and cleaning them and taking them in for checkups will ensure many years of wear.

Nothing beats the time I placed my hefty clown shoes on the counter at the shoe repair shop and the owner deadpanned, Buster Keaton style, "Soooo, you want these stretched."

No matter which kind of shoes you use, remember that the most valuable thing you can do for yourself and for your audience is to invest in your performance and skills. Wearing large clown shoes doesn't make you a funnier or better performer, and without them, you aren't less of a clown than those who have them. Remember Danny Chapman's blue sneakers. The choices are yours; know the alternatives.

"I just want to be known as a clown, because to me that's the height of my profession. It means you can do everything—sing, dance and above all, make people laugh."

— Red Skelton

Chapter 18
Tune-up Time for Touring

Chasing all circuses within a three-hour drive of my home and meeting the clowns and other circus performers was a big part of my life for several years, especially when I lived on the East Coast and was invited to make guest appearances with Clyde Beatty Cole Bros. Circus. Those memorable experiences of being one of the eight burglar clowns chased out of the ring and down the track by a cop clown, and the friendships that developed in clown alley, gave me an even deeper affection for circuses and their performers. Perhaps you, too, have dreamed of running away to join the circus!

I was offered a performance opportunity, along with my partners Steve Rancatore and Trudi Wood, to take my dream one step further. Most of the dates were in Southern California and a few in Nevada.

Producing Clown Steve Rancatore worked two seasons with Red Unit, but for Trudi and me being on tour was a new world.

The difference between a guest appearance and doing a tour an eye-opener, requiring a great deal of forethought and dedication.

I made the commitment to being as healthy and physically fit as possible, which meant going for a check-up, giving up caffeine and sweets, eating better and exercising more frequently. In a nutshell, we were all in training four hours every day for four months prior to the tour. Along with preparing myself physically, I prepared myself mentally. Circus clowning requires a new set of guidelines.

Probably more than any other aspect of this tour, the safety of one another is a top priority. We must be aware of ropes, rigging and ring curbs. All it takes is being too careless one time to get a sprained ankle or worse. Staying out of the workingmen's way as they swiftly move in and out of the ring with props and equipment, yet being available to cover and distract for other acts, is also part of the commitment to being part of the circus.

Since circus performing is worlds apart from parties and picnics, it required many hours of practice. We played fairgrounds, and the audience was a good distance from the ring, so the time spent on physical comedy, all those classic slaps and falls, and projecting with large, clear, crisp body and facial movement was necessary. My time-tested one-liners went on hold in favor of playing big.

This was an exciting adventure as I traded my experiences as a local clown looking from the outside in for a chance to live the circus life.

"I remember in the circus learning that the clown was the prince, the high prince. I always thought that the high prince was the lion or the magician, but the clown is the most important."

— Robert Begnini

Chapter 19
A Spectacle of Big Top Escapades

Life in the Circus Is Not
All Sawdust and Spangles

My two fellow clown troupe members and I picked up our tent trailer in a downpour and set sail from San Francisco for Las Vegas, the first stop on our two-week tour with the All-American Circus produced by Larry Carden. Weeks of preparation were behind us. Now the reality of life on the road and performing in the ring were about to teach me a few lessons. I had guest clowned with Clyde Beatty-Cole Bros. Circus and Hoxie Brothers Circus and thought I knew what circus travels would be like. I was so wrong.

Leslie on the back lot with Arthur, Hoxie Brothers Circus, 1981, Virginia. This is awonderful memory guest clowning with this circus while they were on the East Coast.

The desert sunset was a stunning sight to behold. It had been a long ten-hour drive when we arrived in Las Vegas at 10 p.m. We pulled into an RV Park only to discover we had left the key to the trailer in San Jose, California. We spent two hours breaking in, got to sleep in the wee hours of the morning and hoped that one of our billings in the All-American Circus Program wasn't a sign of things to come. The program promised the audience we would give them "A funny frantic flight of a bumbling brigade!" We opened the next day, Mother's Day, with three back-to-back shows. It was rough going at first as the firing order of the acts varied, and I again learned the value of flexibility.

We eliminated props and tightened gags. The need for resilience and awareness of performers was constant right through to our last shows in Reno. Clowns are parked near the back door of the rings. Reason being, if there is an injury or mishap in the ring, the clowns can run in to distract with a juggling routine or any other funny business. That last afternoon in Reno, Nevada, was so hot, we substituted our usual camera gag with a two-clown juggling act. Good thing because the elephants that followed our act were late, so it was easier to stall with our juggling routine.

Speaking of elephants, did you know on tent and grandstand circuses, clowns live next door to the elephants. Elephants love to pick up dirt with their trunk and fling it over their backs. It keeps the flies off them.

Even though we got used to it, waking up to the sound of leopards panting gives reason to sit up and take notice. I could feel every muscle in my body. Ah, yes, physical comedy as a way of life!

I knew it wouldn't be all sawdust and spangles. In fact, ninety-five percent of life with the circus seems to comprise long hauls on the road, setting up, breaking down, looking for not-too-sleazy-laundromats, sleeping, and repeating the same day after day. I discovered that little things like green grass and shade, after a full day of traveling through heat and dust, took on new meaning.

On our way to Indio, California, we lost a tire and rim from the trailer. We landed in a four-way stop in the middle of nowhere. The nearest town was sixteen miles. Both the cafe and an inspection station were closed, and a fourteen-year-old was running the gas station. Was this the twilight zone?

We got to the circus just in time to set up, get into makeup for the evening show, leave our road hassles at the entrance and, once again, deliver what the program promised: "Those mirthful merry mimics in a flight of felicitous fancy!"

Camaraderie with performers and friends in towns along the way, like trees and shade, kept our spirits up. We got to know Bruce Anderson, a quiet and unassuming man who did a heart-stopping sway pole act, fifty feet above the ground. He did a handstand on one hand at the top of the pole and swayed. He was near retirement age. Bruce was the closer, the highlight of the show. Since we parked forty feet away from Bruce's sway-pole-act, we enjoyed his spectacular performance up close. One evening we started a spaghetti dinner during intermission and shared it with Bruce after the show. We were in clown alley among our wardrobe trunks, enjoying a slight breeze, good food on paper plates, and a new friend.

One of the best parts of the tour was a three-day stand in Santa Ana, California, because I got to meet Bruce "Charlie" Johnson, a fellow *Laugh-Makers* columnist. We commiserated about life on the road as he told us about his two seasons with the Carson and Barnes Circus. It was also great to see another friend, Dena Piraino. Thank heavens for the kindness and hospitality of people like Dena and her family who opened their home and gave clownies away from home the comfort of real beds and hot showers.

I came down with flu and laryngitis in Santa Ana. I saw a doctor and for one day was out of the show except for one gag requiring less physical exertion. It was not fun being sick on the road, and I felt I was letting my partners down. Their understanding and insistence that I rest allowed me to get well enough to be back in the ring the next day. Circus life is demanding enough, but when you're sick it's no picnic.

Despite the hazards of the road, which all traveling performers cope with, it was an honor to work in the circus ring. Running into the ring and seeing the stadiums filled with thousands of smiling faces was a natural high. It was a new experience to hear the Ringmaster announce, "And now let's welcome those ding-a-lings-of-dazzle, The All-American Circus Clowns!" and realize he meant us! The crowds cheered, and we began our gags. It felt different, even a little foreign, but by the end of the tour it felt right, and I enjoyed performing in the ring and the applause. Months of daily training and road hassles were worth it when I heard someone squeal, "They're sooooo funny!"

Being on the road in a circus isn't easy, but I survived it and discovered strengths I didn't know I had. The experience left me with an even greater respect for those hearty souls who made traveling with the circus a way of life—one I know was not for me on a full-time basis. If you, too, have had stars in your eyes about running away to join the circus, I hope my experiences will help you come back to earth. Touring on the circus is not for the faint of heart, and it is not all sawdust and spangles.

*"Keep the circus going inside you, keep it going,
don't take anything too seriously, it'll all work
out in the end."*

— David Niven

Chapter 20
Circus Slanguage

There is jargon that belongs exclusively to the world of the circus. As in any close group, circus lingo evolved from convenience and daily usage. A few expressions were abridged from longer words but carry some of their original flavor; others were coined or invented as the need arose. A number were derived from the Italian and French languages; still others were contributions from the Romanian language of the gypsies. Gradually these words became threads woven into the rich tapestry of the circus.

The following glossary is a compilation of some of the more common terms, including those which have become outdated as the circus changed.

A

Aba-daba—Any dessert that was served in the cookhouse.

Advance Men—Men who go into towns ahead of the circus to put up heralds and posters publicizing the arrival of the circus.

Alfalfa—Paper money.

All Out and Over—Entire performance is concluded.

Annie Oakley—A complimentary ticket or free pass.

Auguste Clown—A clumsy, slapstick clown who wears no traditional costume.

B

Back Door—Performer's entrance to the Big Top.

Bally—A platform used by pitch men to give the crowd an idea of the show to be seen inside.

Ballyhoo—The spiel shouted in front of the sideshow to attract attention.

Banner—The canvas paintings in front of the sideshow depicting the attractions within.

Bibles—Programs or souvenir magazines.

Big Bertha or The Big One—Ringling Brothers and Barnum & Bailey Circus.

Big Top—The main tent used for the performance.

Blowdown—When the tents are blown down by a storm.

Blow Off—The end of the show when the concessionaires come out.

Blues—The general admission seats.

Boss Canvas Man—The man whose job is to decide exactly where and how the tents should be put up at a new circus lot.

Boss Hostler—The man who traveled ahead of the mud shows to mark the way for the caravan; sometimes used to denote the one in charge of all horses in a show.

Bulls—Elephants (whether male or female).

Bunce—Profits.

Butcher—Refreshment merchants, peddler of lemonade, candy, pretzels and other edibles.

C

Calliope—A musical instrument consisting of a series of steam whistles played like an organ; pronounced cally-ope by circus people.

Carpet Clown—A clown who works either among the audience or on arena floor.

Catcher—A member of a trapeze act who catches the flyer after has released himself from the bar in a flying return act.

Cats—Lions, tigers, leopards, panthers.

Cattle Guard—A set of low seats placed in front of the general admission seats to accommodate overflow audiences.

Center Pole or King Pole—The first pole of the tent to be raised. It is about 60 feet high, weighs about a ton and holds the peak of the tent.

Character Clown—A clown who usually dresses in a tramp costume.

Charivari—A noisy whirlwind entrance of clowns; also called shivaree or chivaree.

Cherry Pie—Extra work done by circus personnel for extra pay.

Clem—A fight.

Clown Alley—A section of tent where clowns put on their makeup and store their props.

Clown Stop—A brief appearance of the clowns while the props being changed.

Clown Walk-Around—A parade of clowns during which time they stop and do their acts.

Come-in—The period when the public is entering the arena before the circus begins.

D

Dog and Pony Show—A derisive term for a small circus.

Dona—A woman.

Donikers—Restrooms.

Doors!—Call meaning to let the public in.

Dressage—The art of showing trained horses; animal paces are guided by subtle movements of rider's body.

Dressed—When tickets are distributed so that all sections are filled with no obviously empty areas.

Ducat Grabber—Door tender or ticket collector.

Dukey or Duckie-Box Lunch—The first cookhouse was known as Hotel du Quai. When pronounced quickly it sounded like "dukey" and the name stuck.

Dukey Run—Any circus run longer than an overnight haul.

E

En Ferocite—The term used by European circuses to describe American wild animal acts, as opposed to their "tableau" presentations.

Equestrian Director—Ringmaster (derived from early circuses featuring primarily equestrian performers).

F

Feet Jump-In—Equestrian riding-standing with the feet together, bareback rider jumps from the ground or teeterboard on to back of a running horse.

Fink or Larry—A broken novelty such as a torn balloon.

First of May—A novice performer in his first season on a circus show.

Flatties—People.

Flip-Flaps—The trick of flipping from a standing position to the hands while bareback rider is on a running horse.

Flyers—Aerialists, especially those in flying return acts.

Flying Squadron—The first section of a circus to reach the lot.

Framing a Show—Planning a circus production.

Funambulist—Rope walker. From Latin: "funis" rope, and "ambulare" to walk.

Funny Ropes—Extra ropes added to regular ones, usually at angles, to give extra stability and spread to canvas tent.

G

Gaffer—Circus manager.

Galop—Fast tempo band melodies used in certain exits and entrances.

Gilly—Anyone not connected with the circus; an outsider. See also Towner.

Gilly Wagon—Extra small wagon or cart used to carry light bits of equipment around the lot.

Graft—A piece of work-sometimes easy, sometimes hard.

Grafters—Gamblers who often trail a show.

Grotesque—Type of clown who wears exaggerated costume and carries outlandish props.

Guys—Heavy ropes or cables that help to support poles or high-wire rigging.

H

Harlequin—A clown of the commedia dell'arte who dressed in a diamond-patterned costume and who wore a black mask.

Heralds—Circus advertisements, approximately nine by twenty inches, which can be pasted down or handed out. They are not in color and consist of type and pictures.

Hey Rube!—Traditional battle cry of circus people in fights with townspeople.

High School Horse—A horse who has been taught fancy steps in special riding academies. See also Dressage.

Hits—Places such as walls of grain elevators, barns, buildings, or fences on which heralds and posters were pasted.

Home Run—The trip from Home Sweet Home back to winter quarters.

Home Sweet Home—The last stand of the season when bill posters usually pasted one pack of posters upside down.

Homy—A man. A bona homy is a good man.

Horse—One thousand dollars.

Horse Feed—Poor returns from poor business.

Horse Opery—Any circus (jokingly).

Howdah or Howdy—A seat, often with a canopy, on the back of an elephant or camel.

Human Oddities—Sideshow of abnormal persons.

I

Iron-Jaw Trick—An aerial stunt using a metal bit and apparatus which fits into the performer's mouth. Thus suspended he performs his tricks.

J

Jackpots—Tall tales about the circus.

Jill—A girl.

Joey—A clown (derived from Joseph Grimaldi, a famous clown in England of the 18th century).

Jonah's Luck—Unusually bad weather or mud.

Jump—The distance between performances in different towns.

Jump Stand—An additional booth near the front door used to sell extra tickets during a rush by spectators.

K

Kicking Sawdust—Following the circus or being a part of it.

Kid Show—A sideshow.

Kiester—Wardrobe trunk.

Kinker—Any circus performer (originally only an acrobat).

L

Layout Man—The lot superintendent who decides the location of the various tents.

Lift—The natural bounce which lifts bareback rider from ground to back of a running horse.

Little People—Midgets or dwarfs.

Lot—Land leased by the circus for performances.

Lot Lice—Local townspeople who arrive early to watch unloading of the circus and stay late.

M

Main Guy—Guy rope to hold up center pole in the Big Top.

March, The—The street parade.

Mechanic—The leather safety harness which is worn by lyers in practice sessions and controlled by man below.

Midway—The area near the main entrance where the sideshows are located and concessionaires sell refreshments and souvenirs.

Mud Show—Circus show that traveled overland, not on rails. Named because the wagon wheels were frequently mired in mud.

N

Nanty—Nothing.

O

On the Show—Performers and all others connected to the circus. The term "with" the show is not used.

Opposition Paper—Advertising posters which were put up by competing circuses.

P

Pad Room—Dressing Room. So called because riders hang their pads there.

Paper—Circus posters.

Parlari—Circus people talking.

Perch Act—A balancing act involving use of apparatus upon which one person is performing while being balanced by another.

Picture Gallery—A tattooed man.

Pie-Car—The dining car of a railroad train.

Pitchmen—The salesmen at concessions on the midway.

Planges—Aerialist's body swing overs in which one hand and wrist are placed in padded rope loop.

Ponger—An acrobat.

Possom Belly—Extra storage box attached underneath a work wagon or railway car.

Q

Quarter Poles—Poles which help support the weight of the canvas and take up the slack between center and side poles.

R

Rat Sheets—Advance posters or handbills with negative slant toward the opposition.

Razorbacks—The men who load and unload railroad cars.

Red Wagon—Box office wagon, main office of circus; also money wagon. This was usually painted red though it could be any color.

Rig—To put up aerial rigging.

Rigging—The apparatus used in high wire or aerial acts.

Ring Banks or Curbs—Wooden curbing around the ring.

Ring Barn—Regulation-sized circus ring for practice at winter quarters.

Ring Horse—A horse which performs in the center ring. He is trained to maintain timing despite distractions.

Ring Stock—Circus animals which perform in the show, including horses, llamas, camels, and ponies.

Risley Act—Three acrobats lying on their backs who toss a fourth acrobat from one to the other.

Roll-Ups—Tame U.S. aerial plunges.

Roman Riding—A rider standing on the backs of two horses.

Roper—A cowboy.

Rosinback—Horse used for bareback riding. So named because horses' backs were sprinkled with rosin to prevent rider from slipping.

Roustabout—A circus workman, laborer.

Rubbermen—The men who sell balloons.

S

Safety Loop—The loop part of a web rope into which a performer places her wrist in aerial ballet numbers.

Segue—Music bridge used in changing from one tune to another without stopping.

Shanty or Chandelier—The man who works the lights.

Shill—A man used as a decoy; an employee who stands in line to make the box office look busy and walks in without paying.

Sky Boards—The decorated boards along top of cage wagons used in parades.

Slanger—Trainer of cats.

Sledge Gang—Crew of men who pounded in tent stakes.

Soft Lot—A wet or muddy lot.

Spec—Short form for spectacle. A colorful pageant which is a featured part of the show; formerly used as the opening numbers, now presented before intermission.

Spec Girls—Comedy showgirls who appear in grand spectacle.

Spieler—An announcer.

Splash Boards—Decorated bottom edge of cage wagons used in parades.

Stand—Any town where the circus plays.

Star Backs—More expensive reserved seats.

St. Louis—Doubles or seconds of food. Named because St. Louis engagement was played in two sections.

Strawhouse—A sell-out house. Straw was spread on ground for spectators to sit upon in front of general admission seats.

Swags—Prizes

T

Tableau Wagons—Ornamental parades wagons. Costumed circus performers rode atop them.

Tail Up—Command to an elephant to follow in line.

Talkers—Ticket takers for sideshow; never called barkers.

Tanbark—The shredded bark from trees from which tannin has been extracted; used to cover circus arena ground.

The Big One—Ringling Bros. and Barnum & Bailey Circus.

Toot Up—To get attention of spectators by playing the calliope.

Tops—Tents; for example, dressing tops are where the performers dress for show.

Towners—Townspeople; any outsiders. See also Gilly.

Troupers—Circus entertainers.

Trunk Up—Command to an elephant to raise his trunk in a salute.

Turnaway—A sold-out show.

Twenty-four-hour Man—An advance man who works one day ahead of circus.

W

Wait Brothers Show—Ringling Bros. and Barnum & Bailey Show because their posters read, Wait for the Big Show.

Web—Dangling canvas-covered rope suspended from swivels from the top of the tent.

Web Girl—Female who performs on web in aerial ballet sequence.

Web-Sitter—Ground man who holds or controls the web for aerialists.

Windjammer—A member of a circus band.

With It—An expression meaning loyalty to the show.

Z

Zanies—Clowns.

"Knowing your purpose helps you in using all available resources in achieving your goals."

— Sunday Adelaja

Chapter 21
Clown Resources

Organizations and Education

World Clown Association
http://worldclown.com/

Clowns of America International
https://mycoai.com/

American Clown Academy
https://aca18.com/

International Shrine Clown Association
http://www.shrineclowns.com/index.asp

Western Region Clown Association
https://www.faveconvention.com/

International Clown Week

http://www.internationalclownweek.org/

International Clown Hall of Fame

http://www.theclownmuseum.com/

Clown Camp

https://www.clowncamp.org/

Supplies

Priscilla Mooseburger—Custom costumes, make-up, wigs, skull caps, noses, etc.

https://shop.mooseburger.com/

Clown Costumes

http://www.clowncostumes.com/

The Circus Clown Store

https://the-circus-clown-store.myshopify.com/

Under the Big Top—Unique Clown Supplies
http://bit.ly/2xQCAHj

Props and Supplies

Spears Specialty Shoe Company

http://spearshoes.com/

SkiddlesShoeSmart

https://www.facebook.com/skiddlesshoesmart/
SkiddlesShoeSmart@gmail.com

Crickits Corner—Magic and novelties
www.crickitscorner.com
https://www.facebook.com/Crickitscorner/

LaRocks Fun and Magic Outlet
https://www.larocksmagic.com

Books

The Creativity for Entertainers Trilogy
http://charliethejugglingclown.com/reviews.htm

The World's Funniest Clown Skits, Barry DeChant
https://amzn.to/2LEhBJE

Strutter's Complete Guide to Clown Makeup, Jim
Roberts
https://amzn.to/2LDfx4H

Be a Clown, Mark Stolzenberg
https://amzn.to/2Cb0OyD

Suggested Viewing

Anything with **Avner the Eccentric.** Start with this
http://bit.ly/2v5mAio

George Carl
http://bit.ly/2uKaHM4
http://bit.ly/2vQRXL9

Bob Stromberg
http://bit.ly/2uGlNDw

Bill Irwin
http://bit.ly/1QTLoN0
http://bit.ly/2vf5D5m

Steve and Ryan—Circus clowns
http://bit.ly/2uKlUMQ

Don Christian
http://bit.ly/2u5PlH2

Slapstick Circus
http://bit.ly/2vfg9JQ

Michael Trautman
http://bit.ly/2tKqXLX

Slideshow—Party clowns, Clyde Beatty-Cole Bros. Circus clowns, Hoxie Bros. clowns, and Ringling Bros. and Barnum & Bailey clowns. Late '70s and early '80s. 3:35 minutes.
http://bit.ly/2tgQZZi

*"A satisfied customer is the best
business strategy of all."*

—Michael LeBoeuf

Chapter 22
Bonus: The Performer's Guide
to Smart Business

- No more waiting for the client to finish serving cake and ice cream, to look for their checkbook.

- No more searching large crowds after your show for the contact person to ask for payment.

- No more dealing business matters in the presence of party guests.

- No more last-minute cancellations because the clients changed their mind.

- No more bad checks.

- No more misunderstandings concerning fees, dates and times of performance.

- No more parking a block away (or more) from the performance area.

Don't Be Stiffed Again

If you were ever canceled just before a show or have ever had the misfortune of receiving a bad check for services rendered, you will find "The Performer's Guide to Smart Business" invaluable.

It's difficult to give your all to a performance when business matters aren't handled in advance. The key to good business is preparation and follow-through.

Preparation includes not only what you will provide for the client but what the client must provide in terms of method and time of payment. If your client is sincere in engaging your entertainment services, they will see this method of business as a professional and fair guarantee of reserving their special day and time with you.

Your telephone conversation with a prospective client might go something like this:

PERFORMER: Hello, this is Flower the Clown speaking. May I help you?

CLIENT: Yes. I am planning a birthday party for my daughter and want to know how much you charge.

P: First, please let me know the date of the party so I can check my availability.

C: It's Saturday. Saturday, June first.

P: I have a one o'clock show in Funtown. Where are you located, and how old is your daughter?

C: I live in Ourtown, and my daughter will be five.

P: Great. I can perform at two thirty or three for your guests. Let me tell you something about my show. I offer a thirty- to forty-minute comedy magic show with lots of audience participation throughout. I enjoy featuring the birthday child as the "star" of the show. At the end of the show, I magically produce a live bunny and present your daughter with an eight-by-ten autographed photo of "Flower" and certificate which states she was my Special Assistant throughout the show. Your party guests will all receive prizes, too. My performance fee is $_____. How many children are you planning to invite?

C: We are inviting twenty children, but expect only about fifteen to arrive.

P: It sounds like the perfect size party. What is your daughter's name?

C: Rebecca

P: Well, I would love to entertain Rebecca's party and feature her as the star of the show.

C: Your show sounds like what I am looking for. I'd like to book you. Say, about three p.m. on June 1st?

P: Fine. I would love to. It is my policy to have clients send payment in advance to guarantee and reserve my services at your time and disposal. I will email an invoice with a link for you to pay by credit card or PayPal. Payment is due within twenty-five hours. Once payment is received, I will email reconfirmation with all the information we discussed for the show. Please check for possible errors when you receive the confirmation. I'll need your email address, name, address and phone number.

C: My name is Doris Williams. I live at 123 Fourth Avenue, Ourtown, California. My phone number is (555) 555-5555. My email address is doris.williams@yourmail.com.

P: Thank you. I am looking forward to performing for Rebecca and her friends. Be sure to invite the parents, too. They will enjoy the show as much as the children.

C: That sounds wonderful. Thank you, and I will expect the invoice.

P: Thank you for calling. Goodbye.

C: Goodbye.

When you send the confirmation email after receiving payment, you will want to include promotional material and special instructions for parking, stage conditions, electrical outlets, etc.

The conversation outlines how to handle this style of payment in advance with your clients. Using this as a guide, you will see how the client could be the picnic chairperson for a large corporation. You might discuss meet-and-greet, strolling performance time, and a staged performance. All the basics still apply. Asking the date first to check your availability informs the client you are a busy performer, one who does not waste time. Asking the number of children attending is important if you provide any favors and giveaways.

Letting the client know when you are available to perform shows you are a busy performer once again. When you explain the method of payment, the client will realize that this is your standard procedure. The funds are deposited in a special account and not used until after the show. This protects you should you have to refund payment in case of your incapacitation.

You Booked the Show

Send the invoice and wait for payment from the client. In the meantime, you could receive a call from possible client number 2 for the same day and time, Saturday, June 1, at three p.m.

Call client number 1, Doris Williams, and explain you are calling to inform her that her payment to reserve your show was not received, and you are calling to confirm payment since you have another offer to perform in the same time slot. Sometimes a client will change their mind about the show after the initial contact and instead of calling the performer, they will just not send payment.

It would be unwise to turn down client number 2 on the basis that client number 1 said she wanted to book you and would submit payment.

Only when you receive payment is client number 1's date and time reserved.

Clients don't often avoid payment, but you should protect yourself from losing another engagement.

Special Arrangements

If you perform consistently with a party planner or local restaurant, you might make special arrangements for payment, if the engagements are consistent. These clients should realize your usual policy of advance payment and understand their payment arrangement with you is uncommon.

Large corporations and private enterprises will pay in advance; however, city recreation departments and similar government agencies take the time to appropriate funds, which makes payment in advance unusual. For those instances, you could accept payment at the performance. You should not accept personal checks, but a check from this agency hiring is okay to accept.

One great advantage of requiring payment in advance is that clients are much less likely to call and change the date or time since the show is confirmed with pre-payment and in writing.

When a client calls perhaps less than three days before the event, and you are available to perform, accepting an electronic payment is not appropriate. Payment could be made in cash. Because you may have another show after the cash performance, ask your client to put the cash in an envelope to hand to you on your way in.

Advance Bookings

Should you receive an opportunity to book a show six months to a year in advance, I would advise you to schedule it and inform your client you will be in touch two months prior to the engagement to arrange payment for the show. Should there be any changes to the day or time of the show when you call to discuss payment, you will have enough notice to fill the original time slot with another show.

Emergencies

Most events are scheduled a month or more in advance. Last minute cancellations in these circumstances are uncommon. However, when booking your show into smaller groups such as birthday parties, realize there is such a thing as a valid reason for the client canceling your show. If there is a genuine family emergency, accept their decision to cancel graciously.

At another time, you could reschedule a show with the family at no extra charges. Even if you didn't perform for a birthday, you could offer to perform at a reunion, picnic or holiday party. Use your good judgment about emergency situations. They don't happen often, but when they do, being sympathetic can make it easier on everyone and do good things for your reputation as an entertainer.

Sample Confirmation Email

To: Doris Williams
From: Leslie Ann Akin

Dear Ms. Williams,

Thank you for your payment!

This email confirms receipt of the non-refundable fee of $_____

Flower the Clown is booked to perform at your event:

Type of Performance:

Date:

Time:

Place:

Number of guests expected:

SPECIAL INSTRUCTIONS: Please reserve parking for the performer, accessible to the entrance for transporting props.

If any of the information is in error, please notify me at (555) 555-5555.

Thank you once again, I look forward to entertaining at your special event.

Kind Regards,
Leslie Ann Akin

A Personal Note

"The Performer's Guide to Smart Business" plan has been the cleanest and simplest method of doing business I have discovered. Performing artists will find that this easy-to-follow agreement will ease needless worry before and after performances.

Clients have responded to the method of doing business up front. Financial business is one less concern for both the client and the performer on the day of the show, and it makes the day more enjoyable for everyone.

However, you must keep in mind that a written confirmation of your services and payment in advance demands punctuality and professionalism on your part.

*"I think a simple rule of business is,
if you do the things that are easier first, then
you can actually make a lot
of progress."*

—Mark Zuckerberg

About the Author

Leslie Ann Akin, also known as Flower T. Clown, appeared under the Big Top with Clyde Beatty-Cole Bros., Hoxie Bros., and Great American Circuses and was featured on the nationally syndicated television show *PM Magazine*. In addition to Leslie's busy performing schedule, she was a long-time featured columnist for *The Laugh Makers Magazine*, a national trade publication specifically designed for family-style entertainers. Leslie was the recipient of the coveted EMMETT (Kelly Sr.) AWARD for her contributions to the circus and clowning. Her vast performing experience encompassed charities, embassies, fairs, and even twice at the White House.

Mischief-makers waiting for the train, Gaithersburg, Maryland, 1980. Leslie Ann Akin as Popcorn with Pat McMahan as Satchel.

Leslie performed in Washington, D.C., for many years. After relocating to the San Francisco Bay area, she teamed up with Steve Dawson and Steve Rancatore to form Three Ring

Enterprises, a circus-arts performing and lecturing team dedicated to providing wholesome family entertainment.

After a long and successful career in clowning, Leslie still has a love and passion for sharing her experiences and mentoring new clowns.

Leslie. a strategic brand specialist. owns LeslieTheBrandBoss. com in Lake Oswego, Oregon.

www.ingramcontent.com/pod-product-compliance
Lightning Source LLC
Chambersburg PA
CBHW061145040426
42445CB00013B/1566